Cookir good!

Recipes of Love
Romantic Recipes
by Sweet Romance Reads

Denise Devine

Lyn Cote ✦ Melinda Curtis ✦ Margaret Daley
Denise Devine ✦ Raine English ✦ Donna Fasano
Aileen Fish ✦ Grace Greene ✦ Shanna Hatfield
Milou Koenings ✦ Karen Rock ✦ Roxanne Rustand
Magdalena Scott ✦ Alicia Street ✦ Helen Scott
Taylor ✦Merrillee Whren

Foreword

It's easy to find time to spend with your significant other…

Not.

Okay, for some of us it's hard to make time. But you both have to eat, right? Which means both of you being in the kitchen, both of you sharing a moment. That's where this cookbook comes in.

We're romance writers. We know how to create that moment where your heart melts. And we love food! We've compiled some recipes inspired by our heroes and heroines— everything from snacks to appetizers to entrees and sides to desserts. With each set of recipes, you'll get a small taste of some of the happily-ever-afters we write.

Whether you're new to the kitchen or a gourmet chef, we hope you'll find inspiration in these pages for sweet treats and meal recipes to create a moment with your special someone. After all, in this fast-paced world, everyone deserves a little romance.

Enjoy!

Melinda Curtis

Recipes Inspired by:
"Good Neighbors"
From Two Seasons of Romance,
Short Story Collection
by
Lyn Cote

Here is a reader's take on *Two Seasons of Romance:* "Each story starts with a woman with something weighing on them, whether it is the loss of a spouse, or a divorce, or simply being alone at Christmas... As each story draws to a close, the reader knows that their heroine is going to be getting a new happily ever after." "Good Neighbors" centers on a winter block-party. So here are my fave winter comfort recipes:

Peanut Brittle
Makes 9 x 13-inch pan

2 cups white sugar
1 cup light corn syrup
1 pound of raw peanuts

1. Mix all ingredients in a heavy saucepan and cook until the peanuts turn brown. About 10 – 15 minutes from the time it starts boiling.
2. Remove from heat and beat in 1 teaspoon of baking soda.
3. Pour onto buttered cookie sheet and cool; break up with a covered hammer.

Easy Fudge
Makes 5 pounds.

1 12-ounce can evaporated milk

4 1/2 cups white sugar
8 ounces of marshmallows or 1 jar 13-ounce marshmallow cream
1/2 cup butter or margarine
3 cups chocolate chips semi sweet
1 teaspoon vanilla
2 cups chopped nuts (optional)

1. Combine evaporated milk and sugar in large heavy saucepan; then add marshmallows and butter and cook these ingredients over low or medium heat until melted. Bring mixture to a full boil and stir for four minutes.
2. Remove from heat; stir in chocolate chips until melted.
3. Add vanilla and nuts.
4. Pour into lightly buttered pan. Allow to cool. Can be refrigerated or frozen once it is firm.

Chocolate Peanut Crunch—A great "kid's" recipe
Makes about 3 dozen

6 ounces chocolate chips, semi-sweet
6 ounces peanut butter chips
3 ounces of chow mein noodles
1 cup salted peanuts or mini marshmallows or both

1. Melt chocolate and peanut butter chips in a double boiler.
2. Remove from heat; stir in noodles and peanuts.
3. Then drop by teaspoonfuls onto wax paper. Let stand 20 minutes.

Cut-out Sugar Cookies
Makes 5 dozen

1 cup butter

1 cup sugar
3 1/2 cups flour
2 eggs
2 teaspoons vanilla
2 teaspoons baking powder

1. Cream butter and sugar together.
2. Add eggs and vanilla.
3. Sift flour with baking powder and add to creamed mixture.
4. Chill and rollout and cut into shapes. Bake at 375 degrees F for 8 – 15 minutes.

"Good Neighbors," Two Seasons of Romance Short Story Collection, Excerpt:

"You're new on the block and I know a lot of nice single men right here...."

Refusing to listen to Ethel's eligible bachelor's list, Kate held the phone away from her ear. Since the day Kate moved in, grandmotherly Ethel had proved to be a good neighbor— except for her tendency to match-make. *Why is it everybody's busy wondering whether I'm dating or not?*

A hearty knock at the door saved Kate from coming up with a fresh excuse. "Someone's at the door." She hung up and hurried to answer it.

In the crisp winter sunshine, a blond Viking in a blue ski jacket grinned down at her. "I'm Zak." He handed her a neon green flyer. "I always host the mid-winter block party."

Kate read the flyer, announcing the Annual Winter Block Party Potluck.

"You're new, so I stopped to invite you in person." A little blonde girl peeped around Zak. He moved, urging the child forward. "This is my daughter, Tassie."

Folding her arms around herself against the chill, Kate

smiled. She hadn't met many neighbors because she'd moved in only months ago—right after the first frost when everyone had abandoned their yards for warm hearths.

Small feet pounded up the hallway behind Kate.

"Hi, I'm Jilly!" the most vocal of Kate's twin daughters shouted. Her sister followed close at her heels. "This is Molly." With thick dark hair and pert noses, Molly and Jilly were identical twins and a poignant reminder of their handsome and fun-loving father. About a year ago Josh had passed away, still smiling at his two beloved daughters.

"Hi, girls, I'm Zak and this is Tassie. We're inviting you to our block party."

"What's that?" Jilly asked.

Kate let Zak explain.

"We can go, can't we, Mommy?" Molly looked up with hope.

Kate forced a smile. Was Zak one of those eligible men Ethel had just been listing? She glanced at his hand. No wedding band, but that didn't mean anything. "If we come, should I ask your wife what to bring?"

"I'm not married and anything you bring will be fine." Zak squatted down to be eye-level with the girls. "Everyone wears jeans and fleece. I light my fireplace. We eat, sing songs and play games."

"A winter party sounds like fun." But Kate held back, wanting time to make sure Ethel hadn't prompted Zak's visit. She could hear Ethel, "Zak, Kate's new in the neighborhood. Why don't you hand-deliver the flyer to Kate...."

"Hope you can come and meet everyone." He lifted one hand as though saluting her, then walked down the snow-dusted steps, whistling.

Zak's friendliness had sparked a cheerful glow inside her. Vaguely disconcerted, she closed the door. In the past year, she'd gotten over the worst of her grieving. But ever since she'd lost Josh, everyone had been too eager to match her with someone new. Didn't they understand that no one could replace the man she'd loved?

Lyn Cote Bio

Since her first Love Inspired romance debuted in 1998, Lyn Cote has written over 40 books. A RITA finalist and a Carol Award winner, Lyn writes contemporary romance, romantic suspense and historical. Her homepage blog features "Strong Women, Brave Stories." Visit her website/blog at www.LynCote.com and find her on facebook.com/lyn.cote, goodreads.com/LynCote and twitter.com/LynCote.

Recipes Inspired by:
Always a Bridesmaid
by
Melinda Curtis

In my romantic comedy, *Always a Bridesmaid*, the hero is a chef and the heroine is a master baker prepping for a destination wedding. The recipes for this special meal may end up being served for the rehearsal dinner of Tiff & Jax, the couple featured in *The Wedding Promise*. Or not. You know how wedding prep goes.

Seafood Stuffed Avocado Appetizer
2 Servings

1/2 cup cooked small shrimp
1/2 cup flaked, cooked crabmeat
2 tablespoons cucumber, peeled and diced
1 tablespoon mayonnaise
1 teaspoon chopped fresh parsley
1 pinch salt
1 pinch ground black pepper
1 avocado
1 pinch paprika

1. Gently mix the crab, shrimp, cucumber, mayonnaise, and parsley in a bowl. Season with salt and pepper, stir gently. Cover and chill.
2. When ready to serve, slice the avocado in half lengthwise and remove the pit. Scoop out the avocado, leaving about 1/2 inch on the peel, and slice the flesh. Spoon the seafood into the two avocado halves. Sprinkle each with paprika.

Filet Mignon with Balsamic Glaze
2 Servings

2 4-ounce filet mignon steaks
1/2 teaspoon freshly ground black pepper
Salt, to taste
1/4 cup balsamic vinegar
1/4 cup dry red wine

1. Salt and pepper both sides of each steak.
2. Place non-stick skillet over medium-high heat. When pan is hot, place steaks in pan and cook for 1 minute on each side, or until browned. Reduce heat: medium-low. Add balsamic vinegar and red wine to pan. Cover and cook 4 minutes on each side. Baste with sauce when you turn meat.
3. Remove steaks to warm plates. Top with one tablespoon of glaze each and serve immediately.

Roasted Potatoes with Greens
2 Servings

6 small, quartered red potatoes
2 tablespoons butter
2 cloves garlic, minced
1 tablespoon fresh rosemary, chopped
Sea salt & black ground pepper, to taste
1 cup fresh spinach leaves

1. Preheat oven 400 degrees F (200 degrees C)
2. In a ceramic casserole dish, place the potatoes in a single layer. Over medium heat, melt the butter in a skillet. Add garlic and cook to golden brown. Stir in rosemary.

Remove both when rosemary becomes fragrant. Pour over the potatoes, and season with salt and pepper.
3. Roast uncovered for 30 minutes until the potatoes are fork tender. Toss with the spinach leaves. Return to the oven for 1 – 2 minutes (until spinach wilts).

Parmesan Puffs
2 Servings

1/2 cup milk
1/4 cup margarine
1/2 cup all-purpose flour
2 eggs
3/4 cup fresh grated Parmesan cheese

1. Preheat oven 375 degrees F (190 degrees C). Lightly grease a medium baking sheet.
2. Using a medium saucepan, bring milk and margarine to boil over medium-high heat. Reduce heat to low and stir in flour. Stir vigorously until it thickens enough to form a ball. Remove from heat.
3. Add eggs and beat until smooth. Stir in Parmesan cheese.
4. Drop rounded teaspoonfuls of dough onto baking sheet. Bake 15 minutes or until puffed and golden brown.

Strawberries Flambéed in Vodka with Hot Ice Cream
2 Servings

2 large scoops vanilla ice cream, softened
1 teaspoon hot pepper sauce
2 tablespoons unsalted butter
1/4 cup white sugar
2 cups sliced fresh strawberries

2 ounces vodka
Match

1. In a medium bowl, stir together the ice cream and hot pepper sauce. Place in the freezer until firm.
2. In a small skillet over medium heat, melt butter. Stir in sugar until dissolved, than add the strawberries. Stir occasionally until strawberries are hot. Pour vodka over strawberries, light a match and carefully bring mixture to flame. Let the flames burn out, then remove the pan from the heat.
3. Scoop ice cream into two dishes, top with strawberry vodka sauce, and serve immediately. If you feel creative, serve in martini or margarita glasses.

Always a Bridesmaid Excerpt:

"You're late," Sean grumbled. "You should be prepping your dessert."

"I have plenty of extra time." Words tripped easily off her tongue. "Recall that I don't work for you, Chef. As a courtesy, I sent you a text message when I left Vegas." The closest major airport, a good three hours away.

Sean made a derogatory sound, and reached for a clove of garlic. His movements were culinary poetry, contained power and crisp execution.

What woman wouldn't experience a heart-stopping *ka-thunk* while watching him? Nicole had a fantasy about Sean involving his ability to slice and dice. Flowers, that is. She imagined him visiting a garden, divesting it of blooms, and spreading them over a bed around her. It was a foolish notion given it was about Chef High & Mighty, but it was one she'd been unable to shake.

When Tiff became engaged the first time, Nicole had only known Sean by reputation. She'd agreed to meet Tiff at the reception hall to check out the refrigeration units and there he was – gorgeous and smart, but gruff and grumpy – the antidote to the Siberian Curse. They'd argued over the appropriateness of the kitchen. As a master baker, Nicole had specific requirements that Sean didn't share. She preferred equipment that was top of the line, not new and untested, but not too old either.

Her gaze drifted to Sean, noting the subtle lines that fanned out from his eyes. She'd never noticed those lines before. They didn't make him look old. They made him seem…less Chef High & Mighty and more human.

Human? Must be a trick of the light. Nicole blinked and moved past him to the sink.

Garlic pressed, Sean reached for a sweet potato. He cut it with the quick, steady cadence of a marching band's drummer. "Your text was a little…vague."

"Vague?" Nicole washed her hands. The window over the sink offered a view of the Iron Gate Inn's planked back porch, parking lot, and small winery. All were covered with three feet of softly sloping fresh snow. "I said I was leaving Vegas."

The percussion session ended. Sean didn't look up. His knife paused mid-air. "Do you have a new phone?"

"Yeah. How did you know?" She'd gotten a new phone just yesterday and was still in the love-hate phase, discovering – *or not* – how things worked.

"Check the message you sent me." That holier-than-thou tone of his always hit her wrong, as if someone had put dough in a food processor on puree when it should have been hand-folded.

Nicole pulled out her phone, toggled to his message and read, "*Doodles, I'm live in Vegas now. Are you making porn tonight?*" She raised her phone to heaven, feeling her cheeks heat.

Melinda Curtis Bio

Award winning, USA Today bestseller Melinda Curtis writes the Harmony Valley series of sweet and emotional romances for Harlequin Heartwarming, and the indie pubbed Bridesmaid series. Brenda Novak says: *"Season of Change has found a place on my keeper shelf"*. Melinda also writes independently published, hotter romances as Mel Curtis. Jayne Ann Krentz says of Blue Rules: *"Sharp, sassy, modern version of a screwball comedy from Hollywood's Golden Age except a lot hotter."*

Visit her at www.melindacurtis.net.

Facebook: facebook.com/MelindaCurtisAuthor

Twitter: @MelCurtisAuthor

RECIPES OF LOVE

Recipes Inspired by:
Deadly Holiday
by
Margaret Daley

In *Deadly Holiday* Tory and Jordan shared a Christmas
dinner together. Tory loves to cook and invites Jordan to
celebrate the day with her and her son. Add some friends to
the group and what a fun, delicious way to spend a special
day. Or not. After all, *Deadly Holiday* is a romantic suspense
and no telling what will happen. These dishes can accompany
a honey-glazed spiral ham, baked in its juices.

Cheese Ball
8 Servings

2 large packages of cream cheese
1/4 cup chopped green pepper
8 ounces can crushed pineapple-drained
2 tablespoon finely chopped onions
1 teaspoon seasoned salt
1/4 cup thin sliced ham cut in small pieces
1 cup pecans-finely chopped

1. Squeeze all juice that you can from the pineapple.
2. Mix all the ingredients except the pecans and mold into a
   ball shape.
3. Roll the ball in the pecans and put in the refrigerator until
   ready to serve with crackers.

White Chocolate Eggnog
4 Servings

1/2 gallon of eggnog
2 cups white chocolate chips
Pumpkin pie spice
Whipped cream

1. Melt over medium-low heat white chocolate chips in eggnog.
2. Pour into mugs, and then put the whipped cream and the pumpkin pie spice to taste on top of the drink.

Cornbread Salad
4 to 6 Servings

1 recipe of cornbread
1 envelope ranch dressing mix
1 cup (8 ounces) sour cream
1 cup mayonnaise
2 cans (16 ounces each) pinto beans (rinsed and drained)
2 cups shredded cheddar cheese
10 slices bacon, fried very crispy, and crumbled
2 cans whole kernel corn, drained
1/2 cup each of chopped red bell pepper, green bell pepper, green onions and tomatoes

1. Make up the cornbread, and then let it cool.
2. Combine salad dressing mix, sour cream and mayonnaise until blended, then set aside.
3. Mix tomatoes, bell peppers and onions.
4. Crumble 1/2 the cornbread into a large bowl. Top with half each of beans, tomato mixture, cheese, bacon, corn and dressing mixture. Repeat layer.

5. Cover and chill for at least 3 hours. When ready to serve, stir together.

Zucchini and Yellow Squash Dish
4 to 6 Servings

1 medium to large onion, chopped
1/2 cup of butter (1 stick)
3 zucchinis, chopped in bite-sized pieces
3 yellow squashes, chopped in bite-sized pieces

1. Sauté onion in a skillet in butter until it is cooked.
2. Add zucchini and yellow squash pieces into skillet and stir occasionally over medium to medium-low heat until cooked.
3. Serve with brown rice or alone.

Holiday Surprise
8 Servings

2 cups pretzels
3/4 cup butter melted
1 tablespoon sugar
8 ounces cream cheese
1 cup sugar
12 ounces Cool Whip
6 ounces strawberry gelatin
2 cups boiling water
16 ounces frozen strawberries

1. Crush the pretzels in a plastic bag. Combine pretzels, butter and sugar for the crust. Bake for 8 minutes at 400 degrees F.

2. Layer one: Whip together cream cheese, sugar and Cool Whip. After crust has cooled, put first layer down.
3. Layer two: Melt strawberry gelatin in boiling water. Put frozen strawberries into Jell-O. Set for 10 minutes then pour on top of layer one. Put in refrigerator until ready to serve.

Deadly Holiday Excerpt:
(Shortly after the story begins, Tory Caldwell is driving down a mountain after dropping her son off at a friend's.)

The reckless driver zipped in front of Tory's car, nearly clipping her bumper. She'd barely registered its license plate—HOTSHOT—when it disappeared around the bottom of the S-curve. She breathed easier, knowing at least she didn't have to worry about him riding her tail.

When she hit a straight stretch of the road, she spied the black sports car a hundred yards or so ahead. It was veering toward the drop-off on the right side of the highway. The driver swerved, over-compensated and bounded into the other lane—right toward an older gentleman walking on the shoulder next to the mountain.

The car hit the pedestrian. The man flew into the air.

"No!" Tory screamed.

The older man struck the pavement, his body bouncing.

Stunned, Tory slammed on her brakes and skidded several feet while the driver of the sports car slowed for a few seconds, then revved his engine and sped away.

Tory guided her Jeep to the shoulder, parked, then climbed out, shaking so badly that she held her door until she was steady enough to move. A chilly wind cut through her as she crossed to the man lying face up in a pool of blood. He stared up at her with lifeless eyes.

She knelt, and with a trembling hand, she felt for a pulse at the side of his neck. Nothing. She tried again. Still no pulse.

Then she hovered her fingertips over his slightly open mouth. No breath. She wished she knew CPR, but from the looks of him she didn't think it would have mattered.

She straightened and scanned the area. Deserted. Except for the black sports car, she hadn't seen any other vehicles since she'd started back to Crystal Creek. Not a lot of people lived on the top of this side of the mountain.

As she took one final sweep of her surroundings, she spied a wallet and set of keys not far from the older gentleman. She picked up the brown billfold and flipped it open to see if there was any identification. A photo of a man who looked like the one on the pavement declared the victim was Charles Nelson, seventy-two years old. The address indicated he lived nearby. He had probably been on his way home. Since this was a crime scene, she returned the wallet to where she found it. She shouldn't have touched it in the first place, but at least she could tell the 911 operator who the victim was.

Shivering, she dug into her coat pocket and removed her phone, praying she had driven far enough toward the main highway to get cell reception. No bars. Dead as the man at her feet.

Margaret Daley Bio

Margaret Daley, a USA Today's Bestselling author of over ninety books (five million sold worldwide), has been married for over forty years and is a firm believer in romance and love. When she isn't traveling, she's writing love stories, often with a suspense thread and corralling her three cats that think they rule her household. To find out more about Margaret, visit her website at www.margaretdaley.com.

Recipes inspired by:
This Time Forever
by
Denise Devine

In my inspirational romance, *This Time Forever*, Amber MacKenzie is so desperate to bring her estranged parents back together, she conspires to celebrate her sixteenth birthday by inviting them to an intimate dinner, instead of having her girlfriends over for a sleepover. The only problem is, Amber can't cook. She serves lukewarm soup, wiry spaghetti with cheap sauce, and burnt garlic toast. H-m-m-m...here's a better menu...

Mulled Cider
10 Servings

1 gallon apple cider
4 cinnamon sticks
1 teaspoon whole cloves
Juice of 1 lemon

1.   Simmer gently for 10 minutes.
2.   Remove cinnamon and cloves. Serve warm.

Hot Artichoke Dip
8 Servings

1 cup mozzarella cheese, softened
1 cup Parmesan cheese, shredded
1 cup real mayonnaise
1 can artichokes (not marinated), chopped
2 tablespoons minced onion
1/4 teaspoon minced garlic

1. Mix ingredients together and place in 9 x 9-inch pan.
2. Bake at 350 degrees F for 30 minutes. Serve hot with crackers.

Lasagna
8 Servings

1 pound ground beef
1 small onion, diced
1 jar spaghetti sauce (24-ounce)
1 can diced tomatoes, drained (optional)
1 large carton cottage cheese
2 cups cheddar cheese, shredded
2 cups shredded Parmesan or mozzarella cheese
2 eggs
8 lasagna noodles, cooked and drained

1. Brown ground beef and onion together.
2. Add spaghetti sauce and diced tomatoes and simmer.
3. In large bowl, beat eggs and mix in cottage cheese.
4. Layer in 9 x 13-inch pan:
   4 noodles, 1/2 cottage cheese mix, 1/2 of the sauce and 1 cup of each cheese
5. Repeat.
6. Bake uncovered at 350 degrees F for approximately 90 minutes or until edges are bubbling.

Snicker Cake

1 German chocolate cake mix
1 package of Kraft caramels
1/2 cup (1 stick) of butter
1/3 cup milk

3/4 cup chocolate chips
1 cup chopped nuts

1. Mix cake according to instructions.
2. Pour half of the batter into a 9 x 13-inch greased pan.
3. Bake at 350 degrees F for 20 minutes.
4. Melt caramels with butter and milk.
5. Pour over the thin cake you've just baked.
6. Sprinkle cake with chocolate chips and nuts.
7. Pour the remaining cake batter on top.
8. Bake at 250 degrees F for 20 minutes then 10 minutes at 350 degrees F.
9. Serve warm with whipped cream and/or ice cream.

This Time Forever Excerpt:
   Cash picked up his knife and fork. *Might as well get this over with,* he thought, and began to crosscut the spaghetti. He'd made it past one hurdle, but still had to swallow it. He spied the garlic toast, baked to a golden brown. Now that looked edible—almost tasty. With high hopes, he picked up a piece and took a large bite. It tasted odd. He turned it over. The underside looked like a briquette. He downed his food with a large gulp of water and showed the toast to Libby, flipping it from one side to the other. "How did she manage that?"
   Libby picked up her piece and turned it over. "I'm not sure," she replied, examining it. "Maybe she cranked the heat too high, or maybe she should have set the pan on a higher rack."
   "Maybe she should have ordered out," he whispered and covered everything on his plate with a thick layer of grated cheese, hoping it would salvage the meal. "I would have

gladly picked up the tab. The only food she's ever showed an interest in making is macaroni and cheese, and half the time she scorches that."

Scooping up a forkful, he shoved the cheese-covered spaghetti into his mouth, followed by a large bite of charred toast. He chewed and swallowed, washing it down with a hefty gulp of ice water. Even so, it went down like a chunk of brick.

"It's not so bad," Libby remarked.

Cash paused, his fork suspended in mid-air. "Not if you like rubber spaghetti mixed with scorched sauce and cinders for toast."

"You should have seen the first meal *I* tried to cook," she said, suppressing a chuckle. "I put frozen chicken into a deep frying pan filled with hot oil and it caught on fire. Well, the truth is that it practically blew up the kitchen. The alarm went off and not more than five minutes later, three squads and two hook and ladders showed up at the house."

He stuffed another forkful of cold spaghetti into his mouth while she talked, but the comical expression on her face made him burst out laughing. Unfortunately, the food stuck in his throat, nearly choking him. Laughing and coughing at the same time, he grabbed his water glass.

Libby picked up her napkin and blotted her lips, trying to conceal her amusement.

He caught himself watching her closely again. *Forget it, MacKenzie*, he told himself and went back to work on his meal. *Get your mind off her and concentrate on your food or you'll never get through this.*

ROMANTIC RECIPES BY SWEET ROMANCE READS

Denise Devine Bio
Denise Devine is a USA TODAY bestselling author who has had a passion for books since the second grade when she discovered Little House on the Prairie by Laura Ingalls Wilder. She wrote her first book, a mystery, at age thirteen and has been writing ever since.

She lives on six wooded acres in East Bethel, Minnesota with her husband, Steve, and her three problem (feline) children, Mocha, Lambchop and Tigger. She's presently a cat person, but she loves all animals and they often find their way into her books. Besides reading and writing, Denise also loves to study and travel. For more information, visit her at www.deniseannettedevine.com, facebook.com/deniseannettedevine or pinterest.com/denisedevine1.

RECIPES OF LOVE

Recipes Inspired by:
Cherished Memories
by
Raine English

In my contemporary romance, *Cherished Memories*, the heroine must decide whether or not to sell her childhood home. Memories of the past are making her decision a difficult one, until she runs into an old classmate who wants to turn her quaint cul-de-sac into a high-rise apartment complex. She hopes to thwart his plan by making him fall in love with her. The recipes were inspired by dishes they ordered while on a dinner date.

Asparagus Vinaigrette Appetizer
2 Servings

1/3 cup Italian salad dressing
2 teaspoons chopped parsley
1 teaspoon finely chopped chives
1/2 hard-boiled egg, finely chopped
8 cooked asparagus spears, chilled

1. Mix salad dressing, parsley, chives, and egg. Chill thoroughly.
2. Arrange chilled asparagus on a serving plate lined with lettuce. Garnish with cucumber slices and radish roses.
3. Spoon dressing over asparagus.

Brown Sugar and Ginger Glazed Salmon
2 Servings

1 1/2 teaspoons dark brown sugar

1/2 teaspoon Dijon mustard
1/2 teaspoon soy sauce
1/8 teaspoon ground ginger
Pepper
2 fresh salmon fillets
Toasted sesame seeds (optional)

1. Preheat broiler. Oil broiler rack.
2. In a small bowl, stir together sugar, mustard, soy sauce, and ginger.
3. Pepper fish lightly.
4. Place fish skin side up on rack—6 inches from broiler coils for 3 minutes.
5. Turn fish over. Brush top with sugar mixture. Broil until sugar mixture melts and fish flakes easily with fork.
6. Sprinkle with toasted sesame seeds before serving.

Baked Scallops
2 Servings

8 large sea scallops
4 teaspoons butter
4 teaspoons white wine
4 ounces shredded cheese—Havarti or Monterey Jack
Breadcrumbs

1. Preheat oven to 500 degrees F. Butter casserole dish.
2. Place scallops in casserole dish, dot with butter and add wine. Cover with shredded cheese. Top with breadcrumbs.
3. Bake 10 minutes or until tops are golden.

New Potatoes with Lemon and Chives
2 Servings

5 new potatoes, unpeeled
Salt
2 tablespoons butter or margarine
1/2 teaspoon grated lemon peel
1 teaspoon chopped chives
1 teaspoon lemon juice

1. In a saucepan over medium heat, in 1-inch boiling water, add potatoes and 1/4 teaspoon salt; cover and cook for 15 – 20 minutes, or until fork-tender; drain.
2. Let potatoes cool slightly, then peel and return to saucepan. Salt lightly, add butter or margarine, grated lemon peel, chives, and lemon juice; then heat thoroughly.

Fudgy Brownies with Ice Cream and Chocolate Sauce
Makes about 2 dozen brownies

1 cup butter or margarine
4 squares unsweetened chocolate
2 cups sugar
4 eggs
1 cup all-purpose flour
1 teaspoon vanilla extract
1/2 teaspoon salt

Topping:
Ice cream
Chocolate syrup
Whipped cream

Chopped nuts

1. Preheat oven to 350 degrees F. Grease a 13 x 9-inch baking pan.
2. In a large saucepan, over very low heat, melt butter or margarine and chocolate. Stir constantly. Remove from heat and stir in sugar. Cool slightly.
3. Add eggs, one at a time. Beat until well blended after each addition. Stir in flour, vanilla, and salt.
4. Pour into baking pan.
5. Bake 30 – 35 minutes. Insert a toothpick into center. When it comes out clean, remove from oven.
6. Cool on a wire rack.
7. Cut brownies into pieces.
8. Serve topped with ice cream, chocolate syrup, whipped cream, and chopped nuts.

Cherished Memories Excerpt:

The restaurant was lit with crystal chandeliers, dimmed just the right amount to create an intimate, romantic atmosphere. Too bad she wasn't on a *real* date.

The maître de addressed Ryan. "Good evening, Mr. Cooper. Would you care for your usual table?"

Ryan flashed a dazzling smile. "Yes, Henri. That would be very nice."

The maître de shifted his gaze to Zoe. "Shall I check your coat, miss?"

She wasn't ready for Ryan to see her dress just yet. Per Katie's instructions, the perfect time for the reveal wasn't upon arrival but about fifteen minutes later. "No, thank you. I'm a bit chilly, so I'd like to keep it with me."

"As you wish. Follow me, please." Henri led them to the back of the restaurant and then to a corner booth, far removed from the other tables. "Louis will be right with you, but may I start you off with some wine?"

Ryan didn't hesitate. "We'll have a bottle of your best rosé."

"Excellent choice. I'll have that brought right over."

After Henri left, Ryan leaned in toward her, resting his arms on the table. "You look lovely, by the way. I like your hair like that."

"You mean up?" Zoe ran her hands over the French twist, pushing in a hairpin that had popped out. "No matter how I wear it, I can't seem to stop messing with it," she said with a laugh and then tucked one of the tendrils framing her face behind her ear.

"It's that nervous habit of yours. So tell me, do I make you nervous?"

The way his blue eyes delved into hers made her heart beat faster, but there was no way she was going to admit that to him. "No," she lied. "Of course not. Why would you?"

"I don't know. Wishful thinking, I guess."

She arched a brow at him. Since he was already trying to flirt with her, there was no need to wait to show off her dress. "Where are the restrooms?"

"Head toward the front of the restaurant. Just before the bar, take a right."

"Thanks." She slid off her coat, then got up and walked past him. When she looked over her shoulder, he was staring at her with his mouth agape. The backless dress had provoked the exact response that she'd hoped for. She smiled sexily before strolling away, making sure to swing her hips like Katie had showed her.

This is ridiculous, but hopefully worth it. She'd dated lots of men, and she'd never needed lessons in seduction. Maybe if she'd had them, though, she'd be married by now. Her thoughts drifted to the cad who'd cheated on her. Nah, she was better off single. Much better off. She just had to make sure Ryan didn't discover that she'd sworn off love, or her plan to make him fall for her wouldn't have a chance.

Raine English Bio

USA Today bestselling and award-winning author Raine English writes sweet small-town romances, paranormal, and Gothic romantic suspense. She's a Daphne du Maurier Award winner and a Golden Heart finalist. Her books have made the Top 100 Bestseller lists at both Amazon and Barnes & Noble. For information on all her releases, visit her website at www.RaineEnglish.com.

RECIPES OF LOVE

Recipes Inspired by:
Her Fake Romance
by
Donna Fasano

"Mom! Get a life!" Julia's rebellious, teen-aged daughter's challenge has Julia entering into a comical—and surely doomed—fake romance with her business partner's brother. Ryan agrees to the farce in order to thwart his boss's man-hungry daughter. But when attraction strikes, can love be far behind?

Herb-Stuffed Roasted Cornish Hens
2 Servings

2 Cornish game hens (1 – 1 1/2 pounds each)
12 fresh sage leaves
4 lemon wedges
6 green onions, cut into 2-inch lengths, divided
2 tablespoons butter, melted
2 tablespoon olive oil
1 tablespoon lemon juice
2 garlic cloves, minced
1 teaspoon sea salt
1/2 teaspoon coarsely ground pepper

1. Preheat oven to 375 degrees F. Gently lift skin away from breasts and place sage leaves under skin. Place lemon wedges and the onions in the cavities of the birds. Tuck wings under hens; tie legs together with cotton twine. Place hens in a small, greased roasting pan.
2. Combine melted butter, oil, lemon juice, and garlic; spoon half over hens. Sprinkle hens with salt and pepper. Bake for 30 minutes.

3. Remove hens from oven and brush with remaining butter mixture. Put back into the oven and bake 40 – 45 minutes longer or until a thermometer inserted in thickest part of thigh reads 170 degrees F.
4. Remove hens to a serving platter.

Wild Rice Stuffing
4 to 6 Servings

2 tablespoons butter
1 1/2 cups celery, chopped
1 cup onion, chopped
1 cup uncooked wild rice
2 garlic cloves, minced
4 cups chicken stock
1 1/2 tablespoons fresh sage, minced
1 teaspoon salt (or to taste)
1 teaspoon freshly ground black pepper (or to taste)
1 cup uncooked long-grain brown rice
1/2 cup dried cranberries
1/2 cup dried apricots, chopped
1/2 cup pecans, toasted and chopped

1. Melt butter in a 4-quart pot. Add celery, onion, wild rice, and garlic. Cook until onion is translucent (about 5 minutes), stirring frequently.
2. Add the chicken stock and the sage; bring to a boil. Cover and reduce heat. Simmer for 25 minutes.
3. Add the salt, pepper, and the brown rice, and continue to simmer, covered, for 30 minutes or until all liquid is absorbed.
4. Remove from heat and let sit for 10 minutes. Stir in the cranberries, apricots, and pecans. Taste and adjust seasonings. Serve warm or at room temperature.

Stir-Fried Green Beans
2 to 4 Servings

2 tablespoon extra-virgin olive oil
1/2 pound fresh green beans, stems removed
1 medium onion, thinly sliced
2 cloves garlic, minced
Salt and pepper to taste

1. Heat the oil in a large, heavy skillet. Add green beans and onions. Fry, stirring frequently, for 10 minutes.
2. Add garlic, salt, and pepper, and continue to fry, stirring frequently so garlic doesn't burn, until beans and onions are tender and golden brown, about 15 – 20 minutes.

Coconut Macaroons
6 Servings

14 ounces sweetened flaked coconut
14-ounce can sweetened condensed milk
1 teaspoon vanilla extract
2 extra large egg whites, at room temperature
1/4 teaspoon salt

1. Preheat the oven to 325 degrees F.
2. Combine the coconut, condensed milk, and vanilla in a large bowl.
3. Whip the egg whites and salt on high speed in the bowl of an electric mixer fitted with the whisk attachment until they make soft peaks.
4. Carefully fold the egg whites into the coconut mixture.
5. Drop the batter onto sheet pans lined with parchment paper using either a 1 3/4-inch diameter ice cream scoop, or 2 teaspoons.

6. Bake for 25 – 30 minutes, until golden brown.
7. Cool on wire racks.

Her Fake Romance Excerpt:

Why the heck was Charlotte taking a shower at one o'clock in the afternoon? Didn't she realize they had hens to stuff? Green beans to snap? Vichyssoise to prepare?

Julia went to the refrigerator and pulled open the door. Thank goodness the wild rice stuffing was ready and waiting.

The teakettle whistled, jerking Julia's attention to the stove behind her. Leaving the bowl of stuffing where it sat, she crossed the room and turned off the gas flame.

"What are you trying to do, Charlotte," she murmured under her breath, "burn down your beautiful house?"

Julia heard the shower cut off suddenly. There was a loud thumping of feet. Julia bit back a smile. Her friend and business partner must have remembered the teakettle.

Cocking her head, Julia felt there was something strange about the sound of those footfalls. They sounded heavier than they should have.

Her gaze swiveled toward the stairs, and it seemed that time slowed to a near halt. Bare, muscular calves came into view. Julia's eyes rounded when she saw the steel-like calves.

If those were Charlotte's legs, then the woman had decided to make some sort of hairy fashion statement.

Julia was so taken aback by the sight of the towel-clad man that she couldn't speak. He was in such a rush to reach the kitchen he didn't see her standing there until he was in the middle of the room. Her presence brought him to a sudden, startled halt.

Gee, had she ever seen eyes that blue? And that face. Men this attractive usually graced the covers of glossy fashion magazines. The unbidden thoughts momentarily walloped her like a swift uppercut to the jaw. One corner of her mouth ticked upward in the smallest of appreciative grins. If he were to appear on the cover of any magazine, he'd have to wear something a little less... revealing.

Her eyes blazed a purely spontaneous path down the length of his body. Water droplets clung to his broad shoulders. His well-formed pectorals glistened with damp, golden curls. Her gaze followed the satiny hair as it tapered into a vee just above his taut stomach. She simply couldn't resist taking a quick peek at his well-defined abs. A true six-pack, she surmised.

The fluffy white towel wrapped around his waist exposed a healthy slice of muscular thigh, and before she realized it, she found herself staring at his nicely shaped feet.

He shifted his weight and Julia returned to her senses, realizing the blatant manner in which she'd appraised this complete stranger. She swallowed, her gaze flying to his face as she felt her cheeks suffuse with heat.

Donna Fasano Bio

USA Today Bestseller Donna Fasano has written over thirty romance and women's fiction titles. Her books have won awards and have been translated into nearly two-dozen languages, selling 4 million copies worldwide. Her books are available for Kindle, Nook, Kobo, iBook, trade paperback, and in audio. Learn more about her at DonnaFasano.com.

Recipes Inspired by:
The Cowgirl and the Geek
by
Aileen Fish

My contemporary romance, *The Cowgirl and the Geek*, centers on Katie's work renovating and opening a bar and grill. She is experimenting with recipes, and Juan Diego sees an opportunity to spend time with her by cooking some meals he enjoys. How can you not love a guy who's a gourmet cook, right?

Authentic Bolognese Sauce
8 Servings

2 tablespoons olive oil
1/4 cup butter
1 large yellow onion, finely and evenly diced
4 small (or 2 very large) carrots finely diced
4 stalks celery heart (or 2 large celery stalks) finely diced
4 garlic cloves, very finely diced
4 ounces diced pancetta (1/4-inch cubes)
Sea salt
Freshly ground black pepper
2 pounds lean ground beef (can add veal and pork, if preferred)
1 cup dry white wine
4 tablespoons tomato paste
1 cup beef stock
2 cups milk

1. Heat the butter and the oil together in a large saucepan over medium heat. Add the onion, carrot, celery, garlic and a pinch of salt and sauté for 5 minutes, stirring often.

Add the diced pancetta and cook for about 10 minutes longer, until vegetables are softened and pancetta is golden.
2. Divide meat into three portions. Increase heat to high and add meat to pan one portion at a time, stirring and breaking lumps with a spoon. Cook until brown.
3. Reduce heat to medium, add tomato paste, beef stock and wine, mix well. Add the milk in small amounts until it's completely absorbed. Add salt and pepper to taste, lower heat again and cook slowly for 3 to 4 hours, stirring occasionally and adding milk if it appears to be drying out. You want the sauce to have the consistency of oatmeal when done.
4. Serve with a flat noodle like fettuccini or tagliatelle. (Spaghetti or thin noodles don't hold enough of the sauce!) Top with grated fresh Parmesan.

Grilled Garlic Bread
8 Servings

6 cloves roasted garlic (if roasting your own, purchase 1 head)
1/4 cup olive oil
1 stick butter, softened
Salt and freshly ground pepper
8 slices Italian bread, sliced 1/4-inch thick

Roasted Garlic:
1. Preheat oven to 400 degrees F.
2. Take one head garlic, tear away most of the papery skin, leaving just enough to keep the head intact.
3. Trim the top about 1/4 inch into the garlic cloves.
4. Drizzle with about 1 tablespoon of the olive oil.

5. Wrap in aluminum foil, place on cookie sheet and bake for 40 minutes.

Garlic Bread:
1. Preheat grill. (Can be broiled in oven in winter.)
2. Mash roasted garlic in bowl.
3. Stir in butter and olive oil.
4. Add salt and pepper to taste.
5. Brush one side of bread with butter mix.
6. Grill butter side down until golden.
7. Turn and grill additional 20 seconds. (Skip this step if using broiler.)

Tossed Artichoke Salad
8 Servings

5 cups total torn lettuce and salad greens (romaine, radicchio, butter, arugula, endive, etc.)
1 jar marinated artichoke hearts, drained and chopped
1 cup sliced fresh mushrooms (optional)
1/2 cup Balsamic vinaigrette

1. In a large salad bowl, toss lettuce and greens, artichoke hearts, mushrooms. Just before serving, drizzle with vinaigrette.

Risotto Crab Cakes
8 Servings

Risotto:
2 cans (14 ounces) chicken broth
1 tablespoon butter
2 cloves garlic, minced

1 1/4 cups Arborio rice (other type of rice don't have enough starch)
1 cup shredded mozzarella
Salt and pepper

1. In a saucepan, bring broth to a boil. Reduce heat and simmer.
2. In a sauté pan, melt butter over medium heat. Add garlic and cook for 3 minutes.
3. Add rice and pinch of salt, cook for 1 minute stirring constantly.
4. Add the broth 1/2 cup at a time, stirring constantly, until each portion is absorbed, about 20 minutes total.
5. Remove from heat. Stir in mozzarella. Set aside to cool. (Can be prepared ahead.)

Crab Cakes:
2 cups risotto
2 cups of crabmeat
2 tablespoons of chopped scallions
Cornmeal
1 tablespoon olive oil
1 tablespoon butter

1. In a medium bowl, combine risotto, crabmeat, and scallions. Refrigerate 30 minutes.
2. On a large plate, spread a thin layer of cornmeal.
3. Form meat mixture into 8-12 flattened balls. Press both sides into cornmeal.
4. In a sauté pan, heat butter and oil. Add patties and cook about 3 minutes on each side until golden. Drain on paper towels. Serve immediately.

The Cowgirl and the Geek Excerpt:

Katie Wooten performed one last head count on the calves she'd trailered over from the ranch for the junior rodeo at the White Oak rodeo grounds. "All present and accounted for." She offered a mock salute to Ted, one of the coordinators, and went in search of her BFF, Cheyenne Miller. The next few hours were hers to enjoy.

Cheyenne was wrangling a small herd of her own, but her critters had two legs. She tugged on a boy's sleeve. "Tommy, we do not practice our roping skills on each other."

Katie shook her head and grinned. Her calves were so much easier to control. "I think my charges listen better."

"Yeah, but your charges grow up to be dinner." Cheyenne wrinkled her nose and tucked her thick blonde hair behind one ear. Spreading her arms, she indicated the kids around her. "One of these darling little people might grow up to be the president."

"There's a scary thought. When do you get to turn these guys over to their parents?"

"After the dummy roping." Cheyenne reached out to grab a lasso that flipped into the air. "Tommy! Jilly isn't a dummy. And it's not nice to pretend she is."

Katie clenched her jaw to keep from laughing. Tommy MacCallum was the wildest kid she'd ever met. Seeing him in action made her question having kids of her own someday. Tying him to a chair or caging him was illegal. How did his parents cope?

Shouts rang out from the direction of the calf pen and Katie turned to see what the problem was, her body tensing in preparation to respond as needed. Two men were chasing one of her calves, which was high-tailing it toward her. And the kids. "Get the kids back," she told Cheyenne as she began to run.

The large, big-eyed brown calf looked terrified at all the commotion. Katie anticipated his direction and the muscles in her thighs bunched, ready to jump as it ran near. She watched, waited…closer…now! Katie leaped—and collided with something hard and much larger than a calf.

"Oof!" She landed on top of whatever she hit. Her lungs refused to inflate. Feet pounded past her, voices shouting directions, kids yelling.

"Are you okay?" The body beneath her rolled to one side, easing her to the ground.

"I'm fine. Where's my calf?" She bounced to her feet, searching for her calf. The poor creature stood bawling near a man who clutched the rope looped around the calf's neck. The other end of the rope was in the hands of none other than Tommy MacCallum.

A male voice said, "That kid's pretty good."

Katie suddenly noticed the man who'd collided with her. She ran her gaze slowly up the length of him, all six feet of lean male, clad in jeans and a tan Henley T-shirt that accentuated his pecs. When she met his chocolate brown eyes, he grinned. She didn't. "Juan Diego. What are you doing here?"

Aileen Fish Bio

USA Today Bestselling Author Aileen Fish is an avid quilter and auto racing fan who finds there aren't enough hours in a day/week/lifetime to stay up with her "to do" list. There is always another quilt or story begging to steal away attention from the others. When she has a spare moment, she enjoys spending time with her two daughters and their families, and her fairy princess granddaughter. Her books include The Bridgethorpe Brides series and the Small Town Sweethearts series.

Recipes Inspired by:
Kincaid's Hope
by
Grace Greene

Kincaid's Hope mixes a small-town setting with love and suspense, topped by a zest of Southern flavor—basic fare with a twist contributed by generations of family. In *Kincaid's Hope*, when Beth returns to her hometown of Preston, she finds her old boyfriend Michael still there, along with all the same complications. Then a handsome stranger comes to town on business and treats Beth to an unexpectedly elegant meal. What are your favorite small-town specialties? Maybe potato salad? How about Spoon Bread?

Alfredo-Gorgonzola Tenderloin Sauté
(Delicious, and easier and quicker than creating the sauce from scratch.)
2 Servings

2 4-ounce tenderloin steaks or small tenderloin roast
Italian dressing for marinade (sufficient to cover meat)
Salt and pepper
1 cup Alfredo sauce (your brand of choice)
Gorgonzola cheese shavings
Extra-light tasting olive oil (I use Bertolli)
1 tablespoon butter
1 fresh tomato
1 Portobello mushroom
1/3 cup almond slivers

1. Place meat in dish and cover with Italian dressing to marinade for 2 hours or longer.

4. Put Alfredo sauce in saucepan and heat on low while you slice the mushroom, dice the tomato, and set the almonds close to hand.
5. Remove beef from marinade. If using a small roast, slice across the grain into one-inch slabs.
6. Place one non-stick skillet over medium-high heat. Add thin layer of olive oil and 1 tablespoon of butter. When pan is hot, place mushrooms in pan to brown, flipping as needed. When mushrooms have darkened, push them to the side of the pan and add almonds into the cleared space.
7. Place a second non-stick skillet over medium-high heat with a tablespoon of olive oil. Add beef, and salt and pepper to taste, as beef is flipped until browned on each side. Reduce heat to medium low and cook to desired degree of doneness.
8. In first skillet, push the almonds aside and drop in tomatoes. Mix and sauté the entire mixture for a few minutes, then remove from heat.
9. Place beef on plate, add a few shavings of Gorgonzola, then cover with sautéed mixture, and drizzle hot Alfredo sauce across. Serve immediately.

Serving Note: This dish is usually served with fettuccine, but potatoes (fried, mashed, or baked) will go along beautifully and, of course, potato salad goes with just about anything, but the Red Leaf Green Salad is a perfect match.

Red Leaf Green Salad
(Thanks, Margrit Greene)
2 Servings

1 head of red leaf lettuce
1 small yellow onion, diced

For dressing:
1/8 cup extra-light tasting olive oil
1/8 cup red wine vinegar
Salt and pepper to taste
2 teaspoons sugar

1. Make salad dressing by combining all of the items in a shakable container. Shake briskly and set aside.
2. Hold one hand around lettuce leaves near the top to keep them together and stable. Beginning at the bottom, slice about a half-inch off and discard. From there, slice across (with a very sharp knife) in about 1/4 to 1/3-inch intervals until you reach your hand. Move your hand and discard those loose leaves from the top.
3. Place sliced lettuce in bowl and cover with cold water, then pour water out of bowl. Place your hand in front of the lettuce to prevent it from leaving the bowl. Repeat twice. Do not chill the lettuce or soak it beyond rinsing it and draining the water.
4. Add diced onion to the lettuce. Amount of onion is determined by your preference, but don't overdo.
5. Just before serving, shake dressing briskly, and then pour over the lettuce and toss.

My Sweetheart's Potato Salad
(As taught to my sweetheart by his sweetheart of a mom.)
4 Servings

5 pounds red potatoes
12 ounces (or 1/2 of a 24-ounce jar) Kosher baby dill pickles
2 hardboiled eggs
1/2 cup pickle juice
1/4 cup extra-light tasting olive oil

Hellmann's mayonnaise to desired consistency
Pepper and salt, to taste

1. Wash and put unpeeled potatoes into a deep pot. Cover with water.
2. Turn burner to high and bring to a boil, then reduce heat to sustain a low boil. Remove pot from heat fifty minutes after turning on burner.
3. Drain water from potatoes. Put the potatoes in the refrigerator to cool for at least 6 hours, or even overnight, at least until the potatoes are cold throughout.
4. Peel cold potatoes, slice to preferred size chunks (not too small), and put into a bowl. Add diced pickles and diced eggs. Add salt and pepper to taste. Pour in 1/4 cup pickle juice, 1/4 cup extra-light olive oil. Stir mixture lightly, then add mayonnaise, and then stir again until mayonnaise is evenly distributed. Add more mayonnaise until desired consistency is achieved.
5. Chill potato salad in refrigerator before serving.

Note: Leftover potato salad is even better the next day.

Maude's Spoon Bread
(Grandmother's recipe)
4 Servings

1 cup white corn meal
2 cups boiling water
1 cup whole milk
1 teaspoon salt (I use half that amount)
3 teaspoons baking powder
2 tablespoons softened butter
4 eggs, well-beaten
Optional: 1 teaspoon sugar

1. Preheat oven 400 degrees F. Grease a 2-quart baking dish with butter.
2. Gather the ingredients and have them close at hand.
3. Put 1 cup white corn meal into large bowl and pour 2 cups boiling water over it. Use a large bowl because when you pour the hot water over the corn meal, it will bubble up.
4. Beat in (by hand) the remaining ingredients: milk, salt, baking powder, softened butter, and well-beaten eggs.
5. Bake immediately for 20 – 25 minutes, until golden brown.
6. Serve in baking dish, straight from the oven.

Note: Leftovers reheat well in the microwave.

Kincaid's Hope Excerpt:

Ryan lingered after the meal ended. Their conversation continued beyond dessert as Frank whisked away the last dishes and a soft rattle came from the kitchen as he cleaned up. At one point, her injured ankle began to throb and she must have grimaced because Ryan insisted she prop up her foot. He maneuvered a chair into position and placed her foot on the seat, moving his fingers carefully to avoid putting pressure on her ankle. Beth was speechless.

Ryan spoke. "It's time to say goodnight." But he lingered. After a pause he said, "If I return to Preston, may I visit you? By then, your ankle will be better."

Her cheeks burned. She was pretty sure Ryan was accustomed to this sort of reaction because his voice grew warmer.

"You're flushed. Are you okay?"

She looked up quickly and met his eyes. His dark eyes sparkled in the low light of the lamps. Was he mocking her?

"I'm fine. You're just...not what I expected."

He furrowed his brow. "This meeting was rather last minute, but I thought you were okay with that."

He left an opening for further explanation that mesmerized like a jeweled chasm. Dangerous, but inviting.

Beth answered, "That's not what I meant."

He stared, politely and patiently, waiting her out. She jumped back in to fill the gap.

"I thought you were planning to tear up nature in favor of asphalt. Everything sacrificed for corporate development. I was prepared not to like you."

Ryan laughed out loud. "I'm glad you found the reality better than the assumption."

"Frank's probably finished in the kitchen by now. He must be excruciatingly bored without a TV or anything."

Ryan didn't answer.

She called out, "Frank?"

"I imagine he's done with the cleanup and is out in the car by now, probably relaxing and listening to the radio. Don't worry about Frank. He's fine."

She was reluctant to see Ryan leave, as if a rare and special light would go with him, but she was also ready for him to leave. He should go now while she was still charmed by his charisma.

He left with a handshake. With his departure—the removal of his physical presence—the attraction wasn't extinguished, but it diminished to a more comfortable level. She stood, propped on her crutches, and smiled at the closed door.

Ryan was a man who could make any woman feel desirable simply by looking at her, even one hobbled by crutches and bandages. It was easy to respond to him. Why? Aside from the obvious, that Ryan Markland was a rare, exotic creature who had delightfully and unexpectedly passed a few hours in her catalog home, it was all about the present. There was no inconvenient history to trip over with Ryan as there was with Michael, few expectations, and much less risk to her heart.

Grace Greene Bio

Award winning, USA Today bestseller Grace Greene writes the Emerald Isle, NC Stories, a series of sweet, heart-touching, inspirational romances, as well as the Virginia Country Roads series that includes *Kincaid's Hope, A Stranger in Wynnedower, and Cub Creek,* with lots of mystery and suspense. *Kincaid's Hope* was awarded 4 stars by RT Book Reviews: *"A quiet, backwater town is the setting for intrigue, deception and betrayal in this exceptional offering. Greene's ability to pull the reader into the story and emotionally invest them in the characters makes this book a great read."* Visit her website/blog at www.GraceGreene.com and find her on facebook.com/GraceGreeneBooks, goodreads.com/Grace_Greene and twitter.com/Grace_Greene.

RECIPES OF LOVE

Recipes Inspired by:
Love at the 20-Yard Line
by
Shanna Hatfield

Haven Haggerty is clueless when it comes to men in general and Brody Jackson, star football player, in particular. In the sweet romance, *Love at the 20-Yard Line*, Haven unknowingly charms Brody with her loveable, albeit naïve, personality along with her domestic skills. She is unlike any girl he knows and that's the reason he can't get her out of his head.

Compressed Salad
2 Servings

2 cups of baby lettuce leaves
1 ripe tomato, diced
1/2 cup thinly sliced cucumbers
1/4 cup sliced black olives
1/4 cup sliced pickled beets
2 tablespoons Italian salad dressing
1 tablespoon grated Parmesan cheese, for garnish

1. Mix the lettuce with the dressing.
2. Using individual molds (juice glasses will work if you don't have anything else), layer lettuce with tomatoes, cucumbers, olives, and beets, repeating the layers and pressing down tightly until form is filled. Cover with plastic wrap.
3. Chill for fifteen minutes then remove from mold onto individual plates.
4. Top with a garnish of Parmesan cheese.

Pork Chops
2 Servings

1/2 cup Panko crumbs
1 teaspoon pork rub spices
1 tablespoon all-purpose seasoning
1/2 teaspoon coarse salt
2 pork chops

1. Preheat oven to 425 degrees F (218 degrees C).
2. Mix seasonings, crumbs, and salt in a resealable bag. Shake until blended. Add pork chops, one at a time, to coat. Shake well then place pork chops on a foil-lined baking sheet, lightly coated with non-stick cooking spray.
3. Bake for 20 minutes, until coating is golden brown.

Popovers
2 Servings

1 beaten egg
1/2 cup milk
1 1/2 teaspoons oil
1/2 cup flour
Dash of salt

1. Preheat oven to 400 degrees F (204 degrees C). Spray four custard cups with non-stick cooking spray. Set on a baking sheet and place in the oven as it warms.
2. In a mixing bowl, combine eggs, milk and oil. Add flour and salt. Mix well, beating the batter until smooth on medium speed.
3. Fill the custard cups half-full of the batter. Bake 40 minutes or until very firm.

4. Remove from oven and quickly poke the tops with a fork to let out the steam. Serve immediately.

Fried Apples
2 Servings

1 apple, cut into slices
1 tablespoon butter
1 teaspoon cinnamon
1/4 cup brown sugar

1. Wash apple, core, and slice.
2. Melt butter in a non-stick skillet over medium heat. When melted, add apples, cinnamon, and sugar. Stir well.
3. Cover and simmer until apples are tender, about fifteen minutes, stirring occasionally.

Banana Cake
10 Servings

1 1/2 cups very ripe bananas, mashed
2 teaspoons lemon juice
3 cups all-purpose flour
1 1/2 teaspoons baking soda
1/4 teaspoon salt
3/4 cup butter, softened
2 cups sugar
3 eggs
1 teaspoon vanilla
1 teaspoon banana flavoring
1 1/2 cups milk
Cream cheese frosting

1. Preheat oven to 275 degrees F (135 degrees C). Grease and flour a 9 x 13-inch baking pan.
2. Mash bananas with lemon juice and set aside. Mix flour, baking soda, and salt together, set aside.
3. In a large mixing bowl, cream butter and sugar on medium speed until light and fluffy. Beat in eggs, one at a time, and then blend in vanilla and banana flavoring. Stir in the flour mixture, a little at a time, alternating with the milk.
4. Stir in the bananas then pour into baking pan and bake for 1 hour or until a toothpick inserted in the center comes out clean.
5. Remove from the oven and place directly into the freezer for about an hour. (Place a towel or potholder in your freezer for the pan to rest on as it cools).
6. Remove from the freezer and frost with cream cheese frosting. Serve with caramel ice cream or a drizzle of caramel sauce. If you have any leftovers, keep them refrigerated.

Love at the 20-Yard Line Excerpt:

Seated at one of Haven's favorite tables overlooking the river, Brody smiled at her in a way that made her feel fidgety and uneasy.

The server's arrival pulled Haven out of his entrancing gaze. She spent the next several minutes pretending to study the menu. When the server reappeared with glasses of water and took their orders, she left Haven with nothing to distract her from the extremely appealing Brody Jackson, local football star.

She wasn't one who cared to watch sports on the news, but she'd sat glued to the television when the sportscaster showed a clip of Brody catching a pass at Saturday's game. Watching him on the news confirmed she hadn't imagined how good he looked in his uniform.

In need of something to draw her attention away from his perfect face, she took a notebook and pen out of her bag and placed them in front of her.

"You mentioned an interest in modeling. Is that correct?" Haven asked, prepared to take notes about the types of projects that attracted Brody.

"I did mention I wanted to discuss it," Brody admitted sheepishly.

Puzzled, Haven stared at him as he reached across the table and took her hand in his. Although it made his thoughts jumble, he entirely liked the feel of her hand in his. Far more than he should.

"What I wanted to discuss is that I won't be able to model for you."

"You won't?" Haven asked, confused. She was certain when Brody called to invite her to lunch, he indicated an interest in modeling. As she replayed the conversation in her mind, she recalled him saying he wanted to discuss it, which is what they were doing.

"No. Not with my football contract." Brody experienced pricks of guilt at the look on Haven's face. She attempted to tug her hand away from his, but he held on, rubbing his thumb across her palm soothingly. The movement must have worked because she didn't try to yank it away from him again.

"Then why did you lead me to believe otherwise and why did you bring me here?" Haven eyed him speculatively. "I'm beginning to think you coerced me into meeting you under false pretenses."

Brody knew it was time for a confession. "I'm sorry for misleading you, but I figured if I called and asked you on a date you'd tell me no. I was pretty sure if I called and you thought it was business, you'd agree to meet."

"Trickery, subterfuge, and manipulating the truth. My, my, Mr. Jackson, this doesn't bode well for you." Haven removed her hand from Brody's as the server arrived with their orders. After the girl left them to their meal, Haven looked from her salad to Brody, shaking her head.

She should be angry with him. She should tell him what she thought of his behavior. She should order him to stay far away from her and never call her again.

But she couldn't.

Shanna Hatfield Bio

A hopeless romantic with a bit of sarcasm thrown in for good measure, Shanna Hatfield is a bestselling author of sweet romantic fiction written with a healthy dose of humor. She creates character-driven romances with realistic heroes and heroines. Her historical westerns have been described as *"reminiscent of the era captured by 'Bonanza' and 'The Virginian,'"* while her contemporary works have been called *"laugh-out-loud funny, and a little heart-pumping sexy without being explicit in any way."* In addition to blogging and eating too much chocolate, she is completely smitten with her husband, lovingly known as Captain Cavedweller. Shanna is a member of Western Writers of America, Women Writing the West, and Romance Writers of America.
Follow her online at:
Website: shannahatfield.com/books
Facebook: facebook.com/AuthorShannaHatfield
Twitter: twitter.com/ShannaHatfield
Pinterest: pinterest.com/shannahatfield/boards

Recipes Inspired by:
Reclaiming Home
by
Milou Koenings

In *Reclaiming Home*, Ella Martin spends days keeping vigil over her father who is recovering from surgery in a Boston hospital. Tony Black is touched by her kindness to his brother, who is in the same ward. One night, he insists Ella needs more than coffee for sustenance and offers dinner at an Italian restaurant. Not realizing who he is, she accepts.

A candle-lit dinner, sensuous food and a little red wine could deceive anyone.

Milanese Veal Stew
This is a Milanese riff on the classic Italian osso bucco.
2 Servings

1 pound boneless veal stewing meat, cut in chunks
Salt and pepper to taste
1 1/2 tablespoons flour
1 1/2 tablespoons olive oil
1 medium onion, peeled and chopped
2 carrots, peeled and finely diced
1 rib celery, finely diced
2 cloves garlic, peeled and finely minced
4 ounces of canned stewed tomatoes (half a standard can) not drained.
1/2 cup white wine
1/4 cup tomato sauce
1 bay leaf
Pinch of thyme

Gremolata
1/4 cup chopped fresh parsley
1 tablespoon grated lemon peel
1 clove of garlic, peeled and finely minced

1. Sprinkle the veal with salt and pepper. Dust the pieces on all sides evenly with flour. In a Dutch oven, heat oil. Add the veal and cook until brown on all sides, turning the pieces often, about 7 – 10 minutes. Stir in onion, carrots, celery and 2 garlic cloves. Cook 5 minutes, stirring often.
2. Stir in the tomatoes with the half the liquid from the can, the wine, tomato sauce, bay leaf and thyme and bring to a boil. Reduce the heat to low and simmer, covered, for about 1 1/2 hours, until the veal is tender. Alternatively, cover the pot and cook in the oven, preheated at 350 degrees F, for 1 – 1 1/2 hours.
3. Combine chopped parsley, lemon peel and remaining 1 garlic clove to make the *gremolata*.
4. To serve, remove the bay leaf. Ladle the stew over mashed potatoes, polenta or risotto, and sprinkle with *gremolata*.

Mashed Potatoes with Caramelized Onions
2 Servings

2 tablespoons of olive oil
1 small onion, finely chopped
1/2 pound of potatoes, peeled and cut in small pieces
1 clove garlic, whole

1. In skillet, heat 1 tablespoon of olive oil and cook onion on low heat, stirring frequently, until the onion is caramelized.

2. Meanwhile, put potatoes and garlic clove in pot, cover with water and bring to boil. Lower heat and simmer until potatoes are soft. Set aside a cup of the cooking liquid, and then drain potatoes.
3. Return potatoes to pan, add remaining olive oil and mash. Add reserved cooking liquid as needed to get the desired consistency. Salt and pepper to taste.
4. Mix in the caramelized onions and serve.

Broccoli with Garlic and Oil
2 Servings

1/2 pound of broccoli florets
1 tablespoon olive oil
1 clove garlic, peeled and diced
1/4 cup chopped parsley
1 medium tomato, seeded and chopped

1. Heat oil and garlic in skillet. Add broccoli and stir to coat well with oil. Add parsley and tomato, and salt and pepper to taste.
2. Cover and cook 10 minutes, stirring occasionally, until the broccoli is tender but still crisp.

Lemon Almond Tart
This Italian dessert is filled with contradictions: a sweet and yet tantalizingly tart and creamy filling, light pastry and a hint of crunch. Contradictions that are quintessentially Italian, and of course, always true of life and love as well.

Pastry:
2 eggs, beaten
1/2 cup sugar
Pinch of salt

1 1/2 cup sifted flour
1/2 cup margarine cut in small pieces

Filling:
2 eggs
1/2 cup sugar
Juice from 1 1/2 lemons
Grated peel of 1 1/2 lemons
1/2 cup ground almonds
1 1/2 tablespoons blanched, sliced almonds

1. To make pastry, mix eggs, sugar and salt in bowl until well blended. Add flour bit by bit, mixing well to incorporate before each addition. Using a pastry blender, fingers or two knives, work in margarine until dough forms. Roll dough into a ball, wrap in baking or wax paper and refrigerate for 1 hour.
2. Preheat oven to 375 degrees F. Roll out dough on a lightly floured surface. Press dough in a 9-inch pie plate. Prick holes in the pastry with a fork and bake for 15 minutes.
3. Meanwhile, prepare filling. With an electric mixer, beat eggs and sugar for 7 minutes, until light and creamy. Mix in lemon juice, grated lemon peel, and ground almonds. Pour into prepared pastry shell. Arrange sliced almonds on top. Bake for 30 minutes longer, until filling is set and golden. Cool on wire rack and serve at room temperature.

This makes a full-sized tart, about 8 servings, so there'll be plenty for seconds or to enjoy the next day, when you're reminiscing about your romantic dinner.

Reclaiming Home Excerpt:

"So…you're here building a log cabin?" Ella asked incredulously. "By yourself?"

"What, you don't think I'm capable of building a house by myself? Like you've ever built one," he teased.

"I have, actually."

"You've built a house?"

"Several, in fact. Although not by myself," she admitted.

"Explain." He crossed his arms and leaned back in his chair. Ella told him briefly about the Women Build Hope project.

"It's so gratifying when you know you've made a home for someone," she said. "As opposed to evicting them, like you do. You might have told me you were CB Development, before you let me go on about them. Or was that the point— to spy me out?" She crossed her arms and stared him down.

Tony was looking at her intently, the corner of his mouth lifted in a lopsided smile.

"What?" she asked, indignant that he was once again mocking her.

"Is that what this is about—why you're so angry at me?" he asked. He tilted his head. "You're right, I should have told you as soon as you mentioned it. It wasn't fair of me. It's just that I was having a nice time with you and I didn't want to ruin it." His apology, direct and simple, stumped her. He'd had a nice time? Something inside her uncoiled, a filament of hope.

"But you knew who I was," she finally sputtered. "You said you'd read my blog."

"Guilty as charged. And I did come that evening fully prepared to defend my case, but when you said not to get you started and changed the subject, I wasn't going to go back to it. I was afraid you'd get up and leave me there, having to eat two plates of osso bucco by myself.

"Mind you, that was good osso bucco," Ella teased.

"It was," he grinned. "But your company was better. Would you like me to argue on behalf of CB Dev and the justness of our cause now, or later? Because, once again, I find myself much preferring sitting here with you to talking business." His eyes twinkled and Ella relented.

"Maybe that's because your position is truly indefensible?"

Tony stretched his legs, making himself comfortable. He grinned at her naughtily. "Oh, I think I could defend this position very well."

Milou Koenings Bio

Milou Koenings writes romances because, like chocolate, stories with a happy ending bring more joy into the world and so make it a better place.

Milou loves to connect with readers. She blogs on the 21st monthly at www.sweetromancereads.com, and you can also find her at www.miloukoenings.com, @MilouKoenings on Twitter, facebook.com/MilouKoenings, and plus.google.com/102100526018764125717/posts.

Her novel, *Reclaiming Home, A Green Pines Romance*, is the first of the upcoming *Green Pines* series and is for sale on Amazon.

RECIPES OF LOVE

Recipes Inspired by:
Raising the Stakes
by
Karen Rock

There is something romantic about sharing a meal
outdoors…especially dessert. The couple in my upcoming
April Harlequin Heartwarming novel *Raising the Stakes*,
Liam and Vivie, hike, camp and cook in the Adirondack
Mountains. While they share a mutual love of Button, the
orphaned cub they're raising to return to the wild, they can't
help falling for each other, too. Here are a few decadent
recipes to try when cooking over an open flame:

Banana Boats
8 Servings

8 bananas
1 bag mini-marshmallows
1 bag chocolate/peanut butter/vanilla chips (your choice)
Aluminum foil

1. Take unpeeled bananas and peel down one side of each
    without removing the peel.
2. Make a lengthwise cut in the banana.
3. Fill it with mini-marshmallows and your choice of chips.
4. Replace the peel on the banana and wrap the whole thing
    in foil.
5. Put it over the fire on a grill or directly on hot coals for a
    few minutes to allow the good stuff to melt. Then eat!
    YUMMMM…and some of it is good for you!

Apple Pie Irons
8 Servings

Clamp-shut pie iron
16 slices of bread
Butter- for spreading
1 can of apple pie mix
Powdered sugar
Caramel sauce
Cinnamon
1 pint of vanilla ice cream

1. Butter two slices of bread and put them butter-side down in the iron against the metal.
2. Add pie filling
3. Clamp the irons together.
4. Place the iron in the hottest coal spot possible.
5. Remove after bread is browned.
6. Put on paper plate and sprinkle with powdered sugar, a squirt of caramel and cinnamon on top. Add vanilla ice cream on the side for a decadent wilderness treat.

Blueberry/Orange Muffins Campfire-style
8 Servings

One box blueberry muffin mix
2 eggs
2 tablespoons of oil
16 oranges
Tin foil

RECIPES OF LOVE

1. Stir up a box of blueberry muffin mix following the package directions, (incorporating the eggs and oil).
2. Slice oranges in half and scoop out all of its insides. Save orange flesh for another time, or strain and drink the orange juice.
3. Fill one half of emptied orange with blueberry muffin mix.
4. Cover the filled orange half with the empty orange half and then wrap in at least three layers of aluminum foil.
5. Throw them in the fire. Promise—they will not burn! The orange peel will insulate the muffin mix from burning. The orange peel itself might blacken a little, but the mix in the middle will turn out like a steamed pudding with a delicious orange flavor.
6. Keep turning the aluminum balls over and over in the fire, every minute or so. It usually takes about 10 minutes. Pull them out and check them once in a while until they are firm in the middle. Then unwrap and eat with a spoon! Yum!

Campfire Éclairs
8 Servings

Wooden dowels (2-inch diameter is best)
4 crescent roll dough in tubes
4 containers of chocolate, butterscotch or vanilla pudding
Whipped cream from spray can

1. Soak dowels for a few hours before use.
2. Wrap some crescent roll dough around the soaked part of the dowels.

3. Hold them over the fire until the dough cooks. Don't hold them too close to the fire, or the dough will burn before it cooks through.
4. Then, fill with chocolate, butterscotch or vanilla pudding by putting the pudding in a zip top bag and then cutting one corner out before squeezing the pudding into the crescent roll tubes. Then, top with whipped cream. These are yummy while the dough is warm but the pudding is cool.

Raising the Stakes Excerpt:

A full moon crested Mount Marcy, its pale reflection glimmering on the calmer waters downstream of Marcy Dam. A steady rush of water mingled with the sound of frogs and the faint laughter and guitar strumming from distant campsites. For a moment, Liam's fingers itched to play—a phantom ache from another life. Tonight, the mood was festive, the evening expectant. Yet instead of enjoying himself, he felt restless and stifled. Vivie had shut him out and he wanted in.

He'd grown used to knowing what was on her mind, in her heart. What she planned and what she worried about. Now he'd been left in the dark and was groping for a way to help. But he couldn't do that if she wouldn't open up.

He stared at Vivie, who sat expressionless. Flame-cast shadows pooled beneath her gaunt cheeks and sunken eyes. She'd lost weight since the fire and he noticed an uneaten s'more on a napkin beside her. Was she remembering to take care of herself? Guilt pinched. He should have asserted himself sooner instead of giving her space.

"You asked me once about things I've lost," he began without preamble, watching with satisfaction when her head turned sharply. He had her attention now. As tough as this would be to relay, if it helped her, it was worth reliving.

"Yes." She wrapped her arms around her knees and leaned forward to face him.

"I've mentioned that my father died when I was eleven. My mother's Alzheimer's worsened after that and in a sense I lost her, too."

Vivie moved closer and her leg brushed his. "Does she remember you?"

He squinted at the dark sky, the glittering spots of light brighter than Manhattan. "Sometimes. Though mostly she thinks I'm my twin, Niall. Or even my dad." He'd be seeing his mom next week for Mary Ann's wedding. Would she recognize him this time?

Vivie's small hand twined in his and a deep tenderness took hold. How was it possible that she felt both fragile and strong?

"That's hard. I'm sorry, Liam."

Her face looked otherworldly in the golden flicker of the campfire, the silvery moonlight crowning her brow.

He tightened his fingers in hers, glad for every moment she didn't pull away. His chest expanded, the old dread seizing him as his memory skimmed back ten years.

"I lost fifteen of my battle buddies when under siege in Kunar."

She clutched his other hand, her eyes wide. "Liam. That's awful. I didn't know."

He tightened his fingers around hers and shook his head. "I don't talk about it."

Her nose scrunched. "Ever?"

"Not until now."

"Why are you telling me now?"

He had a lot of reasons, but the deepest truth of all escaped him.

"Because I want you to know me."

"I want that, too," she said at last, and his tense shoulders dropped. He wasn't alone in his feelings. "Tell me."

Karen Rock Bio

Karen Rock is an award-winning YA and adult contemporary romance author. She holds a master's degree in English and worked as an ELA instructor before becoming a full-time writer. With her co-author, Joanne Rock, she's penned the CAMP BOYFRIEND series with Spencer Hill Press under the pseudonym J.K. Rock. The first novel in the series was a finalist in the 2014 Booksellers Best Awards. She also writes contemporary romance for Harlequin Enterprises. Her novel WISH ME TOMORROW has won the 2014 Gayle Wilson Award of Excellence, the 2014 Golden Quill Contest and placed third overall in the Published Maggie Awards. Keep up-to-date on Karen's latest news and contests/giveaways on her Website: www.karenrock.com, her Facebook Page: facebook.com/karenrockwrites and on Twitter at twitter.com/karenrock5 She loves to connect with fellow romance fans!

Recipes inspired by:
Summer at Briar Lake
by
Roxanne Rustand

In *Summer at Briar Lake*, a disillusioned lawyer searching for a quiet life in a small resort town ends up sharing a house with a woman who has a dark past, a troubled daughter and a menagerie of epic proportions. The situation is challenging enough, but add a miniature goat with a penchant for roses and adventure, and an unknown enemy who will stop at nothing to achieve his own goals, and life becomes even more…interesting.

Here's a summer menu that would be just right for a lovely evening on the shore of Briar Lake.

Pecan & Honey Fried Chicken
6 servings

5-6 pounds frying chicken pieces
1 quart buttermilk

Dredging Flour:
2 cups self-rising flour
1 1/2 teaspoons salt
1/2 teaspoon garlic powder
1/2 teaspoon cayenne pepper

Sauce:
1 cup real butter
1/2 cup honey
1/2 cup coarsely chopped pecans
Canola oil for frying

1. Pour buttermilk over chicken pieces in a big bowl. Cover and refrigerate for 2 hours.
2. Mix spices and flour. Pour off buttermilk in the bowl, and then dredge each piece of chicken in the flour.
3. Place the pieces of chicken on racks and let the coating set for 20 minutes.
4. While the chicken is on the racks, melt the butter (not margarine!) in a pan on the stove over low heat. Add honey, bring to a boil, then add pecans and lower the heat to a simmer for 15 minutes. Remove from heat. Don't be tempted to overcook this sauce!
5. Fry chicken in 3/4-inch deep oil, in a 375 degree F electric skillet. Fry until crisp, cooked through, and golden brown—approximately 7 – 8 minutes per side. Set on paper towels when done.
6. Place the chicken on a serving platter, pour the glaze over it, and serve right away.

Best-Ever Potato Salad
12 Servings

8 pounds red potatoes
4 hard cooked eggs, chopped
5 green onions (slice all of the white, and some of the green part)
5 sliced radishes
Salt & pepper to taste

Dressing (blend these ingredients well):
2 cups Hellmann's Original Mayonnaise
2 tablespoons yellow prepared mustard
6 tablespoons sugar
1/4 cup vinegar

1. Cook potatoes until tender. Cool. Peel half of them, and cube them all.
2. Mix using just enough dressing to hold potato salad together. Salt and pepper to taste.
3. Best if refrigerated for several hours before serving.

Briar Lake Layered Salad
12 Servings

Layer the following ingredients in a 9 x 13-inch pan, in this order:
1 head iceberg or 3 bunches of romaine lettuce, chopped
2 stalks celery, sliced
1/4 cup onion, diced small
2 cups frozen, uncooked peas
Dressing (see recipe below)
3/4 pound crisply cooked, crumbled bacon
Shredded sharp cheddar

Dressing:
1/3 cup Hellmann's Original Mayonnaise
1/2 cup sugar
1 cup sour cream
1/4 cup Parmesan cheese

Keep refrigerated until served.

Kahlua Ice Cream Dessert
8-10 Servings

Crust:
2 cups crushed Oreos
1/2 cup melted butter

Filling:
4 pints coffee Häagen-Dazs ice cream softened
1-quart premium chocolate ice cream softened
2 tablespoons powdered instant coffee
1/2 cup coffee liqueur
6 ounces crushed Heath bars

Garnish:
Premium quality commercial chocolate syrup
2 crushed Heath bars

1. Combine crust ingredients and pat moist crumbs into 9"
   springform pan
2. Combine filling ingredients, pour over crust
3. Put in freezer until it is slightly frozen.
4. Drizzle with chocolate sauce and sprinkle with the extra
   crushed Heath bars
5. Cover tightly with foil and freeze

To this menu, add grilled fresh sweet corn, fresh asparagus
broiled with butter and freshly grated Parmesan, and thick
wedges of ripe watermelon. This is a great summer menu!

Summer at Briar Lake Excerpt:

The flame-haired young woman who answered the door
definitely wasn't his aunt Bertie.

Michael fought the urge to step backward and check the
house number intricately worked into the wrought-iron trellis
arched over the entryway. He didn't need to look. The
graceful circular drive in front, the three-story brick home
and every inch of the five-acre grounds were as familiar as
his own house in Chicago.

The diminutive woman guarding the door looked ready to slam it in his face, and from her proprietary stance he instantly knew history had repeated itself.

This one might be infinitely more appealing than the last moocher who had moved in, but he'd make sure she was on her way by nightfall. "I'm here to see Mrs. Wells."

"She's not available."

"I believe she is." He gave the woman a swift, disdainful head-to-toe glance, only to find himself suppressing an unexpected flare of interest. Petite. Delicate features. Wide hazel eyes fringed with dark lashes. He shook off his wayward thoughts and frowned at her.

Apparently Bertie's "housekeepers" had ceased wearing subdued uniforms in favor of flowing caftans in blinding purple hues, black tights and orange tennis shoes.

Then again, knowing his aunt, a flock of Gypsies could have invaded the old estate.

It wouldn't have been difficult for them to do so. Bertie had been adopting people for years. Impoverished students, the homeless—anyone who told her a heartbreaking story could take advantage of her tender heart. She'd given away untold amounts of money, paid tuitions, helped cover the medical bills of total strangers.

Fortunately she'd accepted Michael's prudent advice regarding the management of her investments, or she would have been out on the streets years ago, just like the drifters she was forever trying to help.

Michael sighed. Saving the women in his life from financial ruin was a full-time job.

The woman before him now cast a disparaging glance at his briefcase. "I'm sure Mrs. Wells never buys anything from door-to-door salesmen." With a jangle of colorful bracelets, she started to close the door.

Michael stepped forward and pressed a palm against it. "Hold on, there..."

A deep rumble vibrated through the air with the force of an approaching train. Hot, steamy breath blew against Michael's thigh. Startled, he looked down.

And then he smiled.

Poised to attack a most vulnerable part of his anatomy stood a dog the color and size of a rhino. A very aggressive-looking dog, with teeth like sabers and glittering eyes.

"Baxter, you old fake!"

The dog melted into a massive puddle of ecstasy at his feet. After the requisite ear rub, Michael straightened and held out his hand. "Michael Wells, Bertie's nephew. And you are...?"

The woman frowned. Her gaze focused on his black wavy hair and the widow's peak that the Wells men had inherited for generations past. A dozen old gilt-framed portraits lining the front staircase clearly confirmed his identity.

"Really," she drawled. "Have a picture ID?"

Roxanne Rustand Bio

Award-winning, USA Today bestselling author Roxanne Rustand has written thirty-five traditionally published novels and has independently published four novels. She writes secular sweet romance and romantic suspense, and also writes inspirational romance for Love Inspired. She lives on acreage with her husband, two goofy dogs, six cats and three horses.

Visit me at www.roxannerustand.com or facebook.com/roxanne.rustand.

Recipes Inspired by:
Midnight in Legend, TN
by
Magdalena Scott

Martin McClain, single dad of a teenage son, focuses on easily prepared, hearty meals. Midnight Shelby cooks very little, but brings her artistic talent to the kitchen with this pretty fruit salad. Home-grown fruits and vegetables, locally-sourced meat, fresh baked goods, and homemade jams and jellies are available at the local farmer's market in Legend, Tennessee, each Saturday, spring through autumn. A trip to the farmer's market is a good start for any menu.

Martin's Brunch Casserole
2 to 4 Servings

1 pound sausage, browned and well drained
1 small can of mushrooms, or 1/2 cup fresh mushrooms cleaned and sliced
1 vine-ripened tomato, peeled and diced
1/2 cup prepared baking mix*
1/2 cup milk
4 large eggs
Salt and pepper
Can be easily changed up to something spicier by adding diced peppers or chilies, etc.

1. Grease 8 x 8-inch baking dish. Layer sausage in the bottom, sprinkle mushrooms and then diced tomatoes.
2. Mix baking mix, milk, eggs, salt and pepper together and pour over meat mixture.
3. Bake at 350 degrees F for 40 minutes or until "raised up and slightly golden brown."

ROMANTIC RECIPES BY SWEET ROMANCE READS

*If you don't have a box of prepared baking mix, make your own by mixing together 1/2 cup flour, 3/4 teaspoon baking powder, and 1/8 teaspoon salt. Cut in 1/2 tablespoon butter with a pastry blender.

Fresh Fruit Salad
2 Servings

1/4 cup sugar
1 cup water
Juice of 1/2 lemon
1 orange, peeled and sliced
1/2 cup blueberries
1 banana, peeled and sliced
1/2 cup black grapes
1/2 cup green grapes
1 red apple, cored and diced
1 pear, cored and diced

1. Make syrup by dissolving the sugar in the water over low heat. Bring to a boil for 5 minutes, stirring as needed.
2. Cool and add the lemon juice.
3. Place the prepared fruits in a large bowl and pour syrup over them. Mix well and let stand for 2 – 3 hours.
4. Transfer to a serving bowl. If desired, serve with yogurt. Other fruits such as melon, pineapple, cherries, strawberries, raspberries, peaches and apricots can be added to the fruit salad, or substituted as desired. The salad is most pleasing to the eye when made with fruits of varied colors and shapes.

Morning "Daiquiri"
2 Servings

1 cup orange juice
1 cup pineapple juice
1 banana, quartered
2 ice cubes

1. Frappe in blender; serve immediately in chilled long-stemmed glasses.

Legend by Starlight (Coffee)
Specialty drink of The Emporium in Legend, Tennessee
2 Servings

3 cups of hot, freshly brewed French roast coffee
2 teaspoons Turbinado sugar
1/2 cup Irish Cream
Add, to preference: freshly whipped cream, dark-chocolate stars

2. Pour coffee into two 12-ounce mugs, allowing 1 inch of space at the top.
3. Stir into each mug 1 teaspoon of the sugar and 1/4 cup of the Irish Cream. Spoon onto the top a generous dollop of freshly whipped cream, and sprinkle with tiny dark-chocolate stars. Serve immediately.

Midnight in Legend, TN Excerpt:
After the Christmas Ball…

"Legend by starlight, Miz Shelby. Best viewed from out of the car, if you're up for it."

Midnight pulled her cape around her and slid out of the vehicle. Martin McClain joined her and shut the car door. Then he extended his arm to the cloudless star-filled sky, and the little town glittering below them.

His voice was low. "I've been some places. Not seen the whole world—I'll admit that. But I can't imagine there are many spots prettier than this."

She sighed. "I'd say you're right, Martin. Legend is a cute little town. Legend by starlight is…breathtaking. Add snow, and this would be the perfect Christmas card. In the city, light pollution keeps us from seeing the stars, you know."

"So I hear." He shook his head. "That's an awful shame. A person needs to be able to see the stars, so he has a better sense of his place in this world." He puffed out a breath. "Are you frozen to death yet?"

Midnight had barely kept her teeth from chattering. "Not yet, but it is chilly." She looked up at the sky, out and down at the town. "I hate to leave, though. It's so lovely. Thank you for bringing me up here, Martin." She put a hand on a sleeve of his suit jacket. "Thank you for sharing this with me."

"No problem, Miz Shelby." Martin looked down at her, caught a strand of hair that had escaped, and smoothed it behind her ear. "This is a place the kids come to make out, y'know." He winked. "I've been up here before, but never with anybody like you. You're different, but I like you a lot."

Midnight looked up at him. "I like you too, Martin. You're an interesting person when you're not being all blustery."

Martin leaned down quickly and kissed her lightly on the mouth.

"Had to hurry and do that before I lost my nerve," he said. "You mind?"

"As it happens, no I don't. I imagine I'm more surprised to hear myself say that than you are." Midnight smiled, rose on tiptoe and kissed him back, slowly and thoroughly. His arms came around her and for several minutes there was nothing and no one else in the world but the two of them. Until lights shone on them as another car came along the road.

"Well, hell," Martin muttered, opening Midnight's door so she could climb in. He got in too, and headed the Jeep back down the mountain road.

Neither of them spoke until he parked in the B&B lot.

"Sorry about earlier," he growled. "I was acting like a teenager. Don't know what came over me." Martin stared at the steering wheel.

Obviously he regretted the kiss. Midnight didn't want to feel hurt by that.

"Oh well," she said. "Lovely dinner, beautiful scenery. People get carried away some-times." Her chuckle sounded and felt hollow. "It's no big deal."

"Good. Friends, then?"

"Sure," she said. "Friends."

Magdalena Scott Bio

USA Today Bestselling Author Magdalena Scott writes sweet romance novels that may have you wishing you lived in one of her imaginary towns. Step into Magdalena's world for romance, drama, humor, mystery, and occasional bits of the inexplicable. Magdalena is a lifelong resident of small town America, and shares her otherwise serene studio apartment with Attila, the Kitten from Heck. Sign up for her newsletter, read her blog, or connect on social media by visiting her website: www.magdalenascott.com.

Recipes Inspired by:
The Sweetheart Test
by
Alicia Street

In my romantic comedy, *The Sweetheart Test,* Megan Woods is a can-do manager of a boutique hotel in the resort town of Greenport, New York. Things get interesting when she finds herself romantically caught between two very opposite men. When her workaholic boyfriend forgets her birthday—setting Megan on new course—her best bud, Natalie, consoles her by making her favorite dishes.

Natalie's Lentil Sweet Potato Soup
6 Servings

1 1/4 cups dried green lentils, rinsed
1 quart vegetable broth
1 15-ounce can diced tomatoes with juice
1 medium onion, chopped
2 cloves garlic, minced
2 carrots, chopped
2 celery stalks, chopped
1/2 cup white button mushrooms, chopped
1 cup spinach, chopped, fresh or frozen
1 medium sweet potato, peeled, diced
1 tablespoon brown rice miso (optional)
1/2 teaspoon dried oregano
1/2 teaspoon dried basil
1/2 teaspoon dried rosemary

1. Add all ingredients together in a large soup pot.

2. Bring to a boil, then turn down flame to simmer over medium-low heat. Cook 30 – 40 minutes, stirring frequently.

Honey Mustard Chicken Fingers
8 Servings

2 pounds skinless, boneless chicken breasts, cut into strips

Mustard mixture:
1/2 cup Dijon mustard
1/2 cup honey
1 teaspoon tamari soy sauce
2 tablespoons orange juice
1 clove garlic, minced

Breading:
3 eggs
1 cup whole wheat flour
3 cups whole wheat bread crumbs
1 teaspoon salt

1. Using a glass bowl, stir together mustard, honey, tamari sauce, orange juice, and garlic. After reserving about 1/4 cup for dipping sauce, add chicken to the rest and marinate for 60 minutes.
2. Preheat oven to 450 degrees F. Line baking pan with parchment paper.
3. Beat three eggs in shallow bowl. In another shallow bowl, mix together whole wheat flour and 1/2 teaspoon of salt. In third shallow bowl, mix together breadcrumbs and 1/2 teaspoon salt.

4. Roll each chicken strip in flour mixture. Then dip into beaten egg. Then coat with breadcrumbs. Place on baking sheet.
5. Bake 15 – 18 minutes. Serve with reserved honey mustard sauce.

Arugula and Goat Cheese Salad
4 Servings

1 10-ounce bunch or package of Arugula
1 8-ounce head of Radicchio
4 ounces shelled pecans or walnuts
1 avocado, peeled and sliced
1/2 sweet red pepper, chopped
1/4 cup purple onion, sliced
1 cup grape tomatoes
1 medium pear or apple, cored and cut in thick slices or cubes
6 ounces goat feta cheese
Balsamic vinegar
Extra-virgin olive oil

1. Wash and chop Arugula and Radicchio. Place in large salad bowl.
2. Add in nuts, avocado, red pepper, onion, tomatoes, and pear or apple. Toss well.
3. Crumble feta cheese on top.
4. Dress with vinegar and oil to taste.

Megan's Birthday Cake
Makes one 9x13-inch cake

Frosting:
1 1/2 cups or 3 sticks butter, softened
1 cup unsweetened cocoa

5 cups confectioners' sugar
1/2 cup milk
2 teaspoons vanilla extract.

1. Add cocoa to large bowl and remove any lumps.
2. Cream butter and cocoa powder together until smooth
3. Add sugar and milk, alternating and combining slowly until all is added. Add vanilla extract.

Cake:
1 3/4 cups all-purpose flour
2 cups sugar
3/4 cup unsweetened cocoa powder
2 teaspoons baking powder
2 teaspoons baking soda
1 teaspoon salt
2 eggs
1 cup brewed coffee
1 cup milk
1/2 cup vegetable oil
1 teaspoon vanilla extract

1. Preheat oven to 350 degrees F. Grease two 9-inch round cake pans.
2. Combine flour, sugar, cocoa, baking soda, baking powder, and salt in a large mixing bowl.
3. Add in eggs, coffee, milk, oil, and vanilla. Use electric beater on medium setting for about 2 minutes. Pour into pans.
4. Bake at 350 degrees F for 30 – 40 minutes. Use toothpick to test. Let cool for about 10 minutes, then remove from pans.
5. Frost and stack.

The Sweetheart Test Excerpt:

Megan Woods pulled into the driveway and turned off the music, tunes that never registered in her brain anyway. There was only one thing on her mind. It had been eating at her all day.

Did he remember?

Her hackles rose when she thought of how she'd watched her office door, waiting for him to appear or for a package to arrive.

It was her birthday, darn it! *Gimme a break, Romeo.*

She marched into the two-story clapboard cottage that belonged to her housemate, Natalie D'Alessio, who stood at the stove, adding chopped mushrooms to a lentil soup.

"Smells great." Megan glanced around the kitchen. "Looks like you're making a feast."

"I invited a few of our girl buddies over to celebrate you turning the big three-O."

Which meant Mac wasn't coming to take her out to dinner. How did Natalie know? "Don't tell me Mac called here?"

"No, but when those came, I figured he couldn't make it." She nodded toward the kitchen table across the room.

Megan turned to see a glass vase of pink roses, red tulips, and purple irises—a small lavender envelope tucked into the stems.

So he did remember.

Natalie pulled a pan of chicken fingers from the oven. Megan's favorite. Her housemate was a born nurturer no doubt trying to rescue her from a lonely birthday.

"Don't worry, Natalie. I know most men think birthdays are corny female things. Expecting Mac to drop his business in Boston for the day and fly down to spend it with me isn't fair to him."

She walked to the table. Natalie followed and poured them each a glass of wine from an open bottle of cabernet. She raised her glass. "Happy birthday."

Just as Megan took a sip of her wine, Phil, Natalie's West Highland terrier, came barnstorming into the kitchen in playful pursuit of the newest furry member of the family, Oreo. Megan had found the black-and-white cat combing through their trash in the wee hours last August.

"Easy, you guys," Natalie said, but it was too late. Oreo's table dive knocked over the flowers, and Megan, grabbing for the cat, dropped her glass of wine into the mess.

"Oh no, I've ruined the card." Megan tore it open to see how far the wine penetrated. Although the bottom half was stained beyond reading, what the top half said blew her mind: *Marry me?*

Her phone rang. It was Macaulay.

"How's my girl?"

Nearly breathless, she said, "They're beautiful and the answer's yes."

"That was fast."

"Surprised?"

"Well, the last time I emailed you our latest logo designs for the hotel you took all week to decide. But this is great news. I'll contact—"

"What about the flowers?"

"Flowers?"

"And the proposal?"

"Proposal?"

"Um, listen, I gotta go. I'm celebrating my *birthday,* in case you're interested."

"Oh, right. Sorry, I—"

Megan ended the call and reached for the card, trying to decipher the wine- smudged signature. "If Mac didn't send this—who did?"

Alicia Street Bio

Alicia Street is a *USA Today* bestselling author and a Daphne du Maurier Award winner. She spent many years as a dancer, choreographer and teacher and is a compulsive reader of every genre. Alicia often writes in collaboration with her husband, Roy, and is grateful to have the kind of marriage that proves romance-novel love really exists. Lost in Literature blog says her work has "the perfect amount of giggles, gasps, and anxious page-turning." She loves to connect with readers and answers every email. Find her at her website at aliciastreet-roystreet.com or on Facebook at facebook.com/AliciaRoyStreet or Twitter at twitter.com/AliciaStreet1

RECIPES OF LOVE

Recipes Inspired by:
The Army Doctor's Forever Baby
by
Helen Scott Taylor

In my contemporary romance, *The Army Doctor's Forever Baby*, Sandra has been raised to love cooking, and although she is a doctor, she also longs for a family of her own to care for and pamper. Before George is posted overseas to work as an army doctor, she cooks him a memorable meal in her tiny London apartment.

Butternut Squash Soup
2 Servings

1 medium onion
1 clove of garlic
1 medium sized butternut squash
1 pint of chicken stock
Salt and black pepper to taste

1. Chop the onion into large pieces and crush the garlic clove.
2. Wash the butternut squash then place in an oiled roasting tin with the onion and garlic.
3. Roast for an hour at 365 degrees F (180 degrees C), then spike the squash to check it is soft inside. If the squash requires more cooking, remove the onion and garlic from the roasting tin and cook the squash for another 15 minutes.
4. When the squash is cooked, scoop out the soft flesh, discarding the seeds.

5. Heat the stock, then add the vegetables and use a hand blender to mix to a creamy consistency. Add salt and pepper to taste.
6. Serve with crusty bread.

Pork and Rice Stuffed Peppers
2 Servings

2 large peppers, any color
4 ounces minced pork
1 small onion, finely chopped
Salt and pepper to taste
3 ounces tomato puree
1 ounce feta cheese, cubed
1 ounce cooked white rice
1/2 ounce raisins
1/2 ounce pine nuts

1. Preheat oven to 356 degrees F (180 degrees C). Soak peppers in warm water for 5 minutes.
2. Fry onions until translucent. Fry pork in an oiled skillet until evenly browned then add onions, salt and pepper and tomato puree.
3. Transfer contents of skillet to a bowl then add feta cheese, cooked rice, raisins and pine nuts.
4. Remove the top of the peppers and take out the seeds. Stuff the peppers with the mixture, arrange in a roasting dish and cover with foil.
5. Bake for 30 minutes, then remove foil and continue baking for 10 minutes until stuffing is lightly browned. Serve hot with the Cheesy Sweet Potato Chips.

Cheesy Sweet Potato Chips
2 Servings

1/2 pound sweet potatoes, peeled
1 egg white
1/4 cup Parmesan cheese
1/2 teaspoon fresh rosemary, chopped
Pinch of ground pepper

Spicy Yogurt Dip

1/2 cup plain Greek yogurt
1/4 teaspoon garlic powder
1/4 teaspoon smoked paprika
1/4 teaspoon cumin

1. Preheat oven 425 degrees F (200 degrees C)
2. Grate sweet potato and squeeze the moisture from it between pieces of kitchen towel.
3. In a large bowl put sweet potato, egg white, Parmesan, rosemary and pepper then mix with a wooden spoon.
4. Scoop out tablespoonfuls of mixture onto a greased baking sheet and press flat. Bake for 20 – 30 minutes until chips are dark and crispy at the edges.
5. Add the garlic powder, smoked paprika and cumin to the Greek yogurt, stir then serve as a dip for the chips.

Crème Brûlée
2 Servings

1 cup double cream
1/2 cup full-fat milk
1/2 teaspoon of vanilla essence
3 medium egg yolks

1 ounce caster sugar, plus extra for topping

1. Preheat oven to 320 degrees F (160 degrees C). Put the egg yolks and sugar into a bowl and beat with an electric hand whisk until paler and a bit fluffy.
2. Pour the cream, milk and vanilla essence into a saucepan over medium heat and bring almost to a boil, stirring continuously.
3. Add the hot cream to the eggs and sugar, beating all the time with a wire whisk. Once thoroughly mixed, divide the mixture equally between two ramekin dishes
4. Place the ramekin dishes in a small roasting tin. Fill the roasting tin with water so it reaches halfway up the side of the ramekins. Loosely cover the tin with foil so air can still circulate over the ramekins. Bake for 30 – 35 minutes until the mixture is softly set and wobbles when the dishes are tapped.
5. Cool ramekins completely. It is best to do this overnight in the fridge. Before serving, sprinkle a teaspoon of sugar over the top of each dish and spread it out evenly then use a cook's blowtorch to caramelize it.

The Army Doctor's Forever Baby Excerpt:

On the other side of the village, Saint Cuthbert's Church stood in the middle of the ancient cemetery. They parked on the edge of the road near the tiny thatched kissing gate that led into the churchyard and climbed out of the car.

"What a wonderful place. It looks very old."

"It is. Some of the graves date back to the twelfth century."

A cracked flagstone path led to the heavy oak door. Primroses and buttercups were scattered across the green grass between the gravestones. Sandra clung to George's arm, her thoughts flying as she imagined walking along this path in two weeks beside her father, wearing her lovely lace wedding dress.

George twisted the iron door handle and the latch clanked open. "Gosh. They don't make doors like this anymore." He put a shoulder against the iron-studded oak and pushed. They walked through the medieval entrance porch. The familiar smell of seasoned oak, beeswax polish, and slightly musty fabric pervaded the air.

They were both quiet as they trod the worn red carpet past the font, where she hoped her baby would be baptized. When they reached the nave, they stopped at the head of the aisle.

A serene silence filled the sacred space. Sandra drew in a shuddering breath and released it slowly, letting go all the worries and uncertainties of the past few months. George was home and they would soon be married. Everything was working out perfectly.

"I haven't been in a country church like this since I was at school." George laid a hand on the carved oak leaves and acorns on the bench end of a pew. "There's a peaceful atmosphere in here that you don't find anywhere else."

"I knew you'd like Saint Cuthbert's." This church was part of Sandra's childhood. She'd hoped George would feel as comfortable here as she did.

"It's perfect, darling." He ran his fingertips across her cheek and smiled.

Holding hands, they walked down the aisle and stopped at the step before the altar. Huge fragrant displays of flowers stood on each side.

Will you take George to be your husband? Will you love him, comfort him, honor and protect him, and forsaking all others, be faithful to him as long as you both shall live? The familiar words of the marriage ceremony echoed in her mind. "I do," she whispered.

Sunbeams burst through the stained glass window behind the altar, streaking a rainbow pattern across the carpet at their feet.

George lifted her hand to his lips and kissed her finger beside her engagement ring. "In two weeks you'll be Mrs. Knight. Then in another six months, we'll have our first child. I'm so happy we found each other, love."

"So am I." Sandra wrapped her arms around him and closed her eyes as his strong arms circled her. She was the luckiest woman in the world. Life was perfect and she couldn't be happier.

Helen Scott Taylor Bio

USA Today bestselling author, Helen Scott Taylor, had her first book released in 2009. The Magic Knot, won the American Title contest, was a Golden Heart® finalist, and was chosen as one of Booklist's top ten romances of 2009. Since then, she has published other novels, novellas, and short stories in both the UK and USA.

Recipes Inspired By:
A Place to Call Home
by
Merrillee Whren

These recipes are inspired by the scene from *A Place to Call Home* by Merrillee Whren in which the heroine, Molly Finnerty, and her assistant have prepared some of the dishes they intend to use in the restaurant that is part of the heroine's bed-and-breakfast.

Honey-Glazed Chicken Breasts with Almonds
6 Servings

2 tablespoons lemon juice
1/4 cup soy sauce
1/2 cup honey
1 1/2 teaspoons Dijon mustard
2 minced garlic cloves
1 teaspoon ginger
1/4 teaspoon salt
1/4 teaspoon pepper
6 boneless skinless chicken breast halves

1. Preheat oven to 375 degrees F.
2. Line a baking pan with aluminum foil and spray with nonstick spray.
3. Place the chicken in the pan.
4. In a small bowl, stir together remaining ingredients.
5. Pour half of the mixture over the chicken breasts and refrigerate for an hour.
6. Cover with foil and bake for 20 minutes.
7. Turn chicken breasts over and brush the other side with the remaining honey mixture.

8. Bake uncovered for 20 – 30 or more minutes, brushing occasionally with leftover marinade until juices are clear when chicken is pierced with a knife.
9. Brush with glaze and garnish with sliced almonds before serving.

Asparagus in Cream Sauce
6 Servings

2 pounds fresh asparagus spears
1 tablespoon butter
1 1/2 tablespoons all-purpose flour
1/2 cup chicken broth
1/2 cup half and half
2 tablespoons Dijon mustard
1 teaspoon lemon juice
1/4 teaspoon pepper

1. Cut off tough ends of asparagus.
2. Steam asparagus in a double boiler until crisp-tender.
3. Arrange asparagus spears in serving dish and keep warm.
4. Over low heat, melt butter in a saucepan.
5. Add flour, stirring until the mixture is smooth.
6. Gradually stir in half-and-half and chicken broth. Stir constantly, until thickened and bubbly.
7. Whisk in mustard, lemon juice, and pepper.
8. Spoon sauce over asparagus. Serve immediately.

Potato Soufflé
6 Servings

6 russet potatoes
2 4-ounce containers of whipped cream cheese with chives
1/4 cup sour cream

1/4 cup unsalted butter, melted
2 slightly beaten, large eggs

1. Preheat oven to 400 degrees F and lightly grease a 2-quart soufflé or baking dish.
2. Peel potatoes and quarter.
3. Simmer potatoes in a large saucepan in salted water until tender, about 20 minutes.
4. Drain potatoes and while still warm push through a ricer or food mill, using the medium disk.
5. Beat in remaining ingredients and salt and pepper to taste.
6. Put the potato mixture in the prepared dish. Bake 40 – 45 minutes, or until top is a light golden brown.

Strawberry Chocolate Mousse Cake
12 Servings

1 cup chocolate wafer crumbs
3 tablespoons butter, melted
2 pints fresh strawberries, stemmed and halved
2 ounces semi-sweet chocolate chips
2 tablespoons light corn syrup
1/2 cup orange liqueur
2 1/2 cups whipping cream, divided
1 tablespoon powdered sugar

1. Mix the wafer crumbs and butter thoroughly and press evenly into the bottom of a 9-inch springform pan.
2. With the pointed ends up and cut sides against the pan, stand the strawberry halves around the pan side by side. Set aside. Save the remaining strawberries to garnish the cake.
3. Mix the chocolate chips, corn syrup and orange liqueur in a microwave safe bowl. Microwave on high until the chocolate chips are melted. Whisk the liquids until the

mixture is smooth. Cool.
4. Beat 1 1/2 cups of the whipping cream until it forms stiff peaks.
5. Fold the cool chocolate mixture into the whipped cream and carefully pour into the strawberry lined pan.
6. Refrigerate at least 5 hours or overnight.
7. When ready to serve, whip the remaining whipping cream with the powdered sugar.
8. Release the sides of the pan and arrange the whipped cream on top of the cake and top with the remaining berries.

A Place to Call Home Excerpt:

Setup for excerpt: Molly Finnerty, the heroine of A Place to Call Home, and the hero, Kurt Jansen, are eating a meal that she has prepared and her assistant is serving. He is taste testing the recipes.

Kurt nodded. "This looks great."

"Nice job." Molly smiled up at Kayla. "Presentation is always an intrinsic part of food preparation."

He looked at the chicken breast covered in some kind of glaze and what he thought were sliced almonds, sitting on some leafy green stuff. "Presentation?"

"Yeah. You know, how the food is arranged on the plate. How it's presented." Molly waved a hand over her plate.

Kurt glanced at the plate then looked up at Molly. "Oh. I was noticing how good it looked to eat, not how it was arranged on the plate."

"It all works together."

"Did you learn that in chef's school?"

She nodded. "Would you like to say a blessing for the food?"

"Okay." He realized this was the first time someone had asked him to pray out loud in a long, long time.

He bowed his head and said an audible prayer of thanks for

the food, then silently thanked the Lord for his new job. When he raised his head, Molly was smiling at him. His heart did a crazy little tap dance. Was he going to have more trouble than he thought curbing that attraction? He wished there was a way he could check his emotions at the door when he came into this house.

"Now be honest and tell me what you think." Molly's gray eyes didn't hold that wary look anymore.

Kurt couldn't help smiling. "If I tell you I don't like it, will you fire me?"

"No. I have to have an honest opinion."

"Tell me what I'm eating here."

"Okay." Molly looked over at Kayla. "I'll let you tell him."

"My pleasure." Kayla grinned as she stepped closer. "You have honey-glazed chicken breasts with sliced almonds on a bed of mixed greens, a potato soufflé and asparagus spears in cream sauce."

Kurt tried his best not to wrinkle his nose. "I've never liked asparagus."

"Give it a try. You don't have to eat it if you don't like it." Molly picked up her knife and fork and cut her chicken.

Kurt did the same. A hungry man in his situation didn't turn down anything, even asparagus. After savoring the chicken, he took a bite of the asparagus. It tasted fine. He didn't know whether he liked it because it was good or because he was famished. When he glanced up, Molly was watching him eat. The expression on her face reminded him of a child waiting to find out a test score in school. He wouldn't keep her in suspense.

"You must be a superior cook, because you can even make asparagus taste good."

She laughed. "I hope you're not just being kind."

"I'm not." He shook his head. "Somehow you made this asparagus palatable."

Merrillee Whren Bio

Merrillee Whren is the winner of the 2006 Romantic Times Reviewers' Choice Award for Best Love Inspired of 2006 and the Georgia Romance Writers' Maggie Award for Excellence for her novel, *AN UNEXPECTED BLESSING.*

Merrillee's writing journey has had as many stops along the way as her life's journey. She wrote her first novel while she was in high school and shared it with her friends. However, many years passed before she considered writing anything for publication. Finally in 2003, after writing and revising eight manuscripts, she won the prestigious Romance Writers of America's Golden Heart Award for best, unpublished inspirational manuscript. The following year, she made her first sale to Steeple Hill Books. *THE HEART'S HOMECOMING* was an August 2005 release.

Because she loves stories with happy endings, she is thrilled to be writing inspirational romance, in which the stories have emotional and spiritual happy endings. Merrillee is a member of Romance Writers of America, Novelists, INC., First Coast Romance Writers, Saguaro Romance Writers and American Christian Fiction Writers.

She is married to her own personal hero, her husband of thirty plus years, and has two grown daughters. She has lived near Atlanta, Boston, Dallas, Chicago and Jacksonville but now makes her home in the Arizona desert. She spends her free time playing tennis or walking while she does the plotting for her novels.

RECIPES OF LOVE

About Sweet Romance Reads

Sweet Romance Reads is a group of authors who have joined together to build a community for readers who enjoy a sweeter read. The group includes authors who write sweet romances in a variety of subgenres: Contemporary, Fantasy, Historical, Inspirational, Mystery, Paranormal, Science Fiction, and Suspense.

What constitutes a "sweet" romance? Sweet romances emphasize emotional intimacy and may contain sexual tension, but there are no explicit sexual details. The heat levels range from G to PG.

The authors that have shared recipes in this cookbook are only some who are a part of Sweet Romance Reads. To find more information on the group and its authors visit www.sweetromancereads.com.

Follow Sweet Romance Reads on Facebook at facebook.com/SweetRomanceReads and Twitter at twitter.com/SweetRomanceRds.